Table of Contents

chipalicious
bars

magic cookie bars

1½ cups graham cracker crumbs
½ cup (1 stick) butter or margarine, melted
1 (14-ounce) can EAGLE BRAND® Sweetened Condensed Milk
   (NOT evaporated milk)
2 cups (12 ounces) semisweet chocolate chips
1⅓ cups flaked coconut
1 cup chopped nuts

1. Preheat oven to 350°F (325°F for glass baking dish). In small bowl, combine graham cracker crumbs and butter; mix well. Press crumb mixture firmly on bottom of ungreased 13×9-inch baking pan.

2. Pour EAGLE BRAND® evenly over crumb mixture. Layer evenly with chocolate chips, coconut and nuts; press down firmly with fork.

3. Bake 25 minutes or until lightly browned. Cool. Chill if desired. Cut into bars or diamonds. Store covered at room temperature.

Makes 2 to 3 dozen bars

Prep Time: 10 minutes
Bake Time: 25 minutes

7-layer magic cookie bars: Substitute 1 cup (6 ounces) butterscotch-flavored chips for 1 cup semisweet chocolate chips. (Peanut butter-flavored chips or white chocolate chips can be substituted for butterscotch-flavored chips.)

magic peanut cookie bars: Substitute 2 cups (about ¾ pound) chocolate-covered peanuts for semisweet chocolate chips and chopped nuts.

magic rainbow cookie bars: Substitute 2 cups plain candy-coated chocolate pieces for semisweet chocolate chips.

fudge topped brownies

1 cup (2 sticks) butter or margarine, melted
2 cups sugar
1 cup all-purpose flour
²/₃ cup unsweetened cocoa
¹/₂ teaspoon baking powder
2 eggs
¹/₂ cup milk
3 teaspoons vanilla extract, divided
1 cup chopped nuts (optional)
2 cups (12 ounces) semisweet chocolate chips
1 (14-ounce) can EAGLE BRAND® Sweetened Condensed Milk
    (NOT evaporated milk)
Dash salt

1. Preheat oven to 350°F.

2. In large bowl, combine butter, sugar, flour, cocoa, baking powder, eggs, milk and 1¹/₂ teaspoons vanilla; mix well. Stir in nuts (optional).

3. Spread on bottom of greased 13×9-inch baking pan. Bake 40 minutes or until brownies begin to pull away from sides of pan.

4. In heavy saucepan over low heat, melt chocolate chips with EAGLE BRAND®, remaining 1¹/₂ teaspoons vanilla and salt. Remove from heat.

5. Immediately spread over hot brownies. Cool. Chill if desired. Cut into bars. Store covered at room temperature.

Makes 3 to 3¹/₂ dozen brownies

Prep Time: 10 minutes
Bake Time: 40 minutes

chocolate 'n' oat bars

1 cup all-purpose flour
1 cup quick-cooking oats
3/4 cup firmly packed light brown sugar
1/2 cup (1 stick) butter or margarine, softened
1 (14-ounce) can EAGLE BRAND® Sweetened Condensed Milk
  (NOT evaporated milk)
1 cup chopped nuts
1 cup (6 ounces) semisweet chocolate chips

1. Preheat oven to 350°F (325°F for glass dish). In large bowl, combine flour, oats, brown sugar and butter; mix well. (Mixture will be crumbly.) Reserve 1/2 cup oat mixture and press remainder on bottom of ungreased 13×9-inch baking pan. Bake 10 minutes.

2. Pour EAGLE BRAND® evenly over crust. Sprinkle with nuts and chocolate chips. Top with reserved oat mixture; press down firmly.

3. Bake 25 minutes or until lightly browned. Cool. Chill if desired. Cut into bars. Store leftovers covered at room temperature.

Makes 2 to 3 dozen bars

Prep Time: 15 minutes
Bake Time: 35 minutes

toffee-top cheesecake bars

1¼ cups all-purpose flour
1 cup powdered sugar
½ cup unsweetened cocoa
¼ teaspoon baking soda
¾ cup (1½ sticks) butter or margarine
1 (8-ounce) package cream cheese, softened
1 (14-ounce) can EAGLE BRAND® Sweetened Condensed Milk
    (NOT evaporated milk)
2 eggs
1 teaspoon vanilla extract
1½ cups (8-ounce package) English toffee bits, divided

1. Preheat oven to 350°F. In medium bowl, combine flour, powdered sugar, cocoa and baking soda; cut in butter until mixture is crumbly. Press firmly on bottom of ungreased 13×9-inch baking pan. Bake 15 minutes.

2. In large bowl, beat cream cheese until fluffy. Beat in EAGLE BRAND®, eggs and vanilla until smooth. Stir in 1 cup English toffee bits. Pour mixture over hot crust.

3. Bake 25 minutes or until set and edges just begin to brown.

4. Cool 15 minutes. Sprinkle remaining ½ cup English toffee bits evenly over top. Cool completely. Refrigerate several hours or until cold. Cut into bars. Store leftovers covered in refrigerator.

Makes about 3 dozen bars

Prep Time: 20 minutes
Bake Time: 40 minutes
Cool Time: 15 minutes

s'more bars

1½ cups graham cracker crumbs
½ cup (1 stick) butter or margarine
1 (14-ounce) can EAGLE BRAND® Sweetened Condensed Milk
   (NOT evaporated milk)
1 cup (6 ounces) milk chocolate or semisweet chocolate chips
1 cup chopped nuts (optional)
1 cup miniature marshmallows

1. Preheat oven to 350°F (325°F for glass dish). In small bowl, combine graham cracker crumbs and butter; mix well. Press crumb mixture firmly on bottom of ungreased 13×9-inch baking pan.

2. Pour EAGLE BRAND® evenly over crumb mixture. Layer evenly with chocolate chips, nuts (optional) and marshmallows; press down firmly with fork.

3. Bake 25 minutes or until lightly browned. Remove from oven; sprinkle with marshmallows. Return to oven. Bake 2 minutes more. Cool. Chill if desired. Cut into bars. Store covered at room temperature.

Makes 2 to 3 dozen bars

Prep Time: 15 minutes
Bake Time: 27 minutes

Keep in mind the type of pan you choose for a particular recipe will effect the baking time. The darker the pan, the quicker the bars will bake. The lighter the pan, the slower the bars will bake.

white chocolate squares

  2 cups (12 ounces) white chocolate chips, divided
  ¼ cup (½ stick) butter or margarine
  2 cups all-purpose flour
  ½ teaspoon baking powder
  1 (14-ounce) can EAGLE BRAND® Sweetened Condensed Milk
     (NOT evaporated milk)
  1 egg
  1 teaspoon vanilla extract
  1 cup chopped pecans, toasted
     Powdered sugar

1. Preheat oven to 350°F.

2. In large saucepan over low heat, melt 1 cup white chocolate chips and butter. Stir in flour and baking powder until blended. Stir in EAGLE BRAND®, egg and vanilla. Stir in pecans and remaining white chocolate chips. Spoon mixture into greased 13×9-inch baking pan.

3. Bake 20 to 25 minutes. Cool. Chill if desired. Sprinkle with powdered sugar; cut into squares. Store covered at room temperature.

Makes 2 dozen squares

Prep Time: 15 minutes
Bake Time: 20 to 25 minutes

fudge-filled bars

2 cups (12 ounces) semisweet chocolate chips
2 tablespoons butter or margarine
1 (14-ounce) can EAGLE BRAND® Sweetened Condensed Milk
   (NOT evaporated milk)
2 teaspoons vanilla extract
2 (18-ounce) packages refrigerated cookie dough (oatmeal-
   chocolate chip, chocolate chip or sugar cookie dough)

1. Preheat oven to 350°F.

2. In heavy saucepan over medium heat, melt chocolate chips and butter with EAGLE BRAND®, stirring often. Remove from heat; stir in vanilla. Cool 15 minutes.

3. Using floured hands, press 1½ packages of cookie dough on bottom of ungreased 15×10-inch baking pan. Pour cooled chocolate mixture evenly over dough. Crumble remaining dough over chocolate mixture.

4. Bake 25 to 30 minutes. Cool. Chill if desired. Cut into bars. Store covered at room temperature. *Makes 4 dozen bars*

Prep Time: 20 minutes
Bake Time: 25 to 30 minutes

 If you want to trim the fat in any EAGLE BRAND® recipe, just use EAGLE BRAND® Fat Free or Low Fat Sweetened Condensed Milk instead of the original EAGLE BRAND®.

chocolate nut bars

1¾ cups graham cracker crumbs
½ cup (1 stick) butter or margarine, melted
2 cups (12 ounces) semisweet chocolate chips, divided
1 (14-ounce) can EAGLE BRAND® Sweetened Condensed Milk
    (NOT evaporated milk)
1 teaspoon vanilla extract
1 cup chopped nuts

1. Preheat oven to 375°F. In medium bowl, combine graham cracker crumbs and butter; press firmly on bottom of ungreased 13×9-inch baking pan. Bake 8 minutes. Reduce oven temperature to 350°F.

2. In small saucepan over low heat, melt 1 cup chocolate chips with EAGLE BRAND® and vanilla. Spread chocolate mixture over baked crust. Top with remaining 1 cup chocolate chips and nuts; press down firmly.

3. Bake 25 to 30 minutes. Cool. Chill if desired. Cut into bars. Store loosely covered at room temperature.   *Makes 2 to 3 dozen bars*

Prep Time: 10 minutes
Bake Time: 33 to 38 minutes

candy bar bars

¾ cup (1½ sticks) butter or margarine, softened
¼ cup peanut butter
1 cup firmly packed light brown sugar
1 teaspoon baking soda
2 cups quick-cooking oats
1½ cups all-purpose flour
1 egg
1 (14-ounce) can EAGLE BRAND® Sweetened Condensed Milk
   (NOT evaporated milk)
4 cups chopped candy bars (such as chocolate-covered caramel-
   topped nougat bars with peanuts, chocolate-covered crisp
   wafers, chocolate-covered caramel-topped cookie bars or
   chocolate-covered peanut butter cups)

1. Preheat oven to 350°F. In large bowl, combine butter and peanut butter until smooth. Add brown sugar and baking soda; beat well. Stir in oats and flour. Reserve 1¾ cups crumb mixture.

2. Stir egg into remaining peanut butter mixture; press firmly on bottom of ungreased 15×10-inch baking pan. Bake 15 minutes.

3. Pour EAGLE BRAND® evenly over baked crust. Stir together reserved peanut butter mixture and candy bar pieces; sprinkle evenly over top.

4. Bake 25 minutes or until golden brown. Cool. Chill if desired. Cut into bars. Store leftovers loosely covered at room temperature.

Makes 4 dozen bars

Prep Time: 15 minutes
Bake Time: 40 minutes

double chocolate fantasy bars

1 (18.25-ounce) package chocolate cake mix
¼ cup vegetable oil
1 egg
1 cup chopped nuts
1 (14-ounce) can EAGLE BRAND® Sweetened Condensed Milk
   (NOT evaporated milk)
1 cup (6 ounces) semisweet chocolate chips
1 teaspoon vanilla extract
   Dash salt

1. Preheat oven to 350°F. In large bowl, combine cake mix, oil and egg; beat at medium speed until crumbly. Stir in nuts. Reserve 1½ cups crumb mixture. Press remaining crumb mixture firmly on bottom of greased 13×9-inch baking pan.

2. In small saucepan over medium heat, combine EAGLE BRAND®, chocolate chips, vanilla and salt. Cook and stir until chips melt.

3. Pour chocolate mixture evenly over prepared crust. Sprinkle reserved crumb mixture evenly over top.

4. Bake 25 to 30 minutes or until set. Cool. Chill if desired. Cut into bars. Store loosely covered at room temperature.

Makes 3 dozen bars

Prep Time: 15 minutes
Bake Time: 25 to 30 minutes

toffee bars

(pictured on page 21)

1 cup quick-cooking oats
½ cup all-purpose flour
½ cup firmly packed light brown sugar
½ cup finely chopped walnuts
½ cup (1 stick) butter or margarine, melted and divided
¼ teaspoon baking soda
1 (14-ounce) can EAGLE BRAND® Sweetened Condensed Milk
  (NOT evaporated milk)
2 teaspoons vanilla extract
2 cups (12 ounces) semisweet chocolate chips
Additional chopped walnuts (optional)

1. Preheat oven to 350°F. In large bowl, combine oats, flour, brown sugar, walnuts, 6 tablespoons butter and baking soda. Press firmly on bottom of greased 13×9-inch baking pan. Bake 10 to 15 minutes or until lightly browned.

2. In medium saucepan over medium heat, combine remaining 2 tablespoons butter and EAGLE BRAND®. Cook and stir until mixture thickens slightly, about 15 minutes. Remove from heat; stir in vanilla. Pour evenly over baked crust. Bake 10 to 15 minutes or until golden brown.

3. Remove from oven; immediately sprinkle with chocolate chips. Let stand 1 minute; spread chocolate chips while still warm. Garnish with additional walnuts (optional); press down firmly. Cool. Chill if desired. Cut into bars. Store tightly covered at room temperature.

Makes 2 to 3 dozen bars

Prep Time: 10 minutes
Bake Time: 20 to 30 minutes

almond fudge-topped shortbread

    1 cup (2 sticks) butter or margarine, softened
    $\frac{1}{2}$ cup powdered sugar
    $\frac{1}{4}$ teaspoon salt
    1$\frac{1}{4}$ cups all-purpose flour
    2 cups (12 ounces) semisweet chocolate chips
    1 (14-ounce) can EAGLE BRAND® Sweetened Condensed Milk
       (NOT evaporated milk)
    $\frac{1}{2}$ teaspoon almond extract
    Sliced almonds, toasted

1. Preheat oven to 350°F. Grease 13×9-inch baking pan. In large bowl, beat butter, powdered sugar and salt until fluffy. Add flour; mix well.

2. With floured hands, press evenly into prepared pan. Bake 20 to 25 minutes or until lightly browned.

3. In heavy saucepan over low heat, melt chocolate chips with EAGLE BRAND®, stirring constantly. Remove from heat; stir in almond extract. Spread evenly over shortbread.

4. Garnish with almonds; press down firmly. Chill 3 hours or until firm. Cut into bars. Store leftovers covered at room temperature.

Makes 2 to 3 dozen bars

Prep Time: 15 minutes
Bake Time: 20 to 25 minutes

chocolate mint cheesecake bars

 2 cups finely crushed crème-filled chocolate sandwich cookie
   crumbs (about 24 cookies)
 $\frac{1}{2}$ cup (1 stick) butter or margarine, melted
 1 (8-ounce) package cream cheese, softened
 1 (14-ounce) can EAGLE BRAND® Sweetened Condensed Milk
   (NOT evaporated milk)
 2 eggs
 1 tablespoon peppermint extract
 $\frac{1}{2}$ cup semisweet chocolate chips
 2 teaspoons shortening
 14 thin crème de menthe candies, chopped

1. Preheat oven to 325°F. In medium bowl, combine cookie crumbs and butter; blend well. Press crumb mixture firmly on bottom of ungreased 9-inch square baking pan. Bake 6 minutes. Cool.

2. In medium bowl, beat cream cheese until fluffy. Gradually beat in EAGLE BRAND®, eggs and peppermint extract until smooth. Pour over cooled cookie base.

3. Bake 25 to 30 minutes. Cool 20 minutes; chill. Just before serving, in heavy saucepan over low heat, melt chocolate chips and shortening. Drizzle over top of chilled cheesecake bars. Sprinkle chopped crème de menthe candies over top. Cut into bars. Store leftovers covered in refrigerator.   *Makes 1½ to 2 dozen bars*

Prep Time: 15 minutes
Bake Time: 31 to 36 minutes

double delicious cookie bars

1½ cups graham cracker crumbs
½ cup (1 stick) butter or margarine
1 (14-ounce) can EAGLE BRAND® Sweetened Condensed Milk
   (NOT evaporated milk)
1 cup (6 ounces) semisweet chocolate chips*
1 cup (6 ounces) peanut butter-flavored chips*

*Butterscotch-flavored chips or white chocolate chips can be substituted for the semisweet chocolate chips and/or the peanut butter-flavored chips.

1. Preheat oven to 350°F (325°F for glass dish). In small bowl, combine graham cracker crumbs and butter; mix well. Press crumb mixture firmly on bottom of ungreased 13×9-inch baking pan.

2. Pour EAGLE BRAND® evenly over crumb mixture. Layer evenly with chocolate chips and peanut butter chips; press down firmly with fork.

3. Bake 25 to 30 minutes or until lightly browned. Cool. Chill if desired. Cut into bars. Store leftovers covered at room temperature.

Makes 2 to 3 dozen bars

Prep Time: 10 minutes
Bake Time: 25 to 30 minutes

drop cookies

choco-peanut butter-brickle cookies

1 (14-ounce) can EAGLE BRAND® Sweetened Condensed Milk
   (NOT evaporated milk)
1 cup crunchy peanut butter
2 eggs
1 teaspoon vanilla extract
1½ cups all-purpose flour
1 teaspoon baking soda
½ teaspoon baking powder
½ teaspoon salt
1 cup (6 ounces) semisweet chocolate chips
1 cup chocolate-covered toffee bits or almond brickle chips

1. Preheat oven to 350°F. In large bowl, beat EAGLE BRAND®, peanut butter, eggs and vanilla until well blended.

2. In medium bowl, combine flour, baking soda, baking powder and salt. Add to peanut butter mixture; beat until blended. Stir in chocolate chips and toffee bits. Drop by heaping tablespoonfuls onto lightly greased baking sheets.

3. Bake 12 minutes or until lightly browned. Cool. Store leftovers tightly covered at room temperature.   *Makes 3 dozen cookies*

Prep Time: 15 minutes
Bake Time: 12 minutes

holiday treasure cookies

1½ cups graham cracker crumbs
½ cup all-purpose flour
2 teaspoons baking powder
1 (14-ounce) can EAGLE BRAND® Sweetened Condensed Milk
(NOT evaporated milk)
½ cup (1 stick) butter or margarine, softened
1⅓ cups flaked coconut
1¾ cups (10 ounces) mini kisses, milk chocolate baking pieces or
semisweet chocolate baking pieces
1 cup red and green holiday baking bits

1. Preheat oven to 375°F. In medium bowl, combine graham cracker crumbs, flour and baking powder; set aside.

2. Beat EAGLE BRAND® and butter until smooth; add reserved crumb mixture, mixing well. Stir in coconut, chocolate pieces and holiday baking bits. Drop by rounded teaspoonfuls onto greased cookie sheets.

3. Bake 7 to 9 minutes or until lightly browned. Cool 1 minute; transfer from cookie sheet to wire rack. Cool. Store leftovers tightly covered at room temperature. 　·　　　　　　　*Makes about 5 dozen cookies*

Prep Time: 10 minutes
Bake Time: 7 to 9 minutes

coconut macaroons

1 (14-ounce) can EAGLE BRAND® Sweetened Condensed Milk
    (NOT evaporated milk)
1 egg white, whipped
2 teaspoons vanilla extract
1½ teaspoons almond extract
1 (14-ounce) package flaked coconut

1. Preheat oven to 325°F. Set aside.

2. In large bowl, combine EAGLE BRAND®, egg white, extracts and coconut; mix well. Drop by rounded teaspoonfuls onto foil-lined, greased and floured baking sheets; slightly flatten each mound with a spoon.

3. Bake 15 to 17 minutes or until lightly browned around edges. Immediately remove from baking sheets (macaroons will stick if allowed to cool on baking sheets); cool on wire racks. Store loosely covered at room temperature. *Makes about 4 dozen cookies*

Prep Time: 10 minutes
Bake Time: 15 to 17 minutes

double chocolate cookies

2 cups biscuit baking mix
1 (14-ounce) can EAGLE BRAND® Sweetened Condensed Milk
   (NOT evaporated milk)
8 (1-ounce) squares semisweet chocolate, melted *or*
   1 (12-ounce) package semisweet chocolate chips, melted
3 tablespoons butter or margarine, melted
1 egg
1 teaspoon vanilla extract
1 cup (6 ounces) white chocolate chips
1 cup chopped nuts

1. Preheat oven to 350°F.

2. In large bowl, combine baking mix, EAGLE BRAND®, semisweet chocolate, butter, egg and vanilla; beat until smooth. Stir in white chocolate chips and nuts. Drop by rounded teaspoonfuls 2 inches apart onto ungreased baking sheets.

3. Bake 10 minutes or until tops are slightly crusted (do not overbake). Cool. Store leftovers tightly covered at room temperature.

Makes about 5¹/₂ dozen cookies

Prep Time: 15 minutes
Bake Time: 10 minutes

Checking the doneness of chocolate cookies may be difficult at first. You should rely on the baking time noted in the recipe for your first batch. Simply adjust the time accordingly for each additional batch. For next time, be sure to note on the recipe the best baking time for your particular oven.

chocolate chip treasure cookies

1½ cups graham cracker crumbs
½ cup all-purpose flour
2 teaspoons baking powder
1 (14-ounce) can EAGLE BRAND® Sweetened Condensed Milk
    (NOT evaporated milk)
½ cup (1 stick) butter or margarine, softened
2 cups (12 ounces) semisweet chocolate chips
1⅓ cups flaked coconut
1 cup chopped walnuts

1. Preheat oven to 375°F. In small bowl, combine graham cracker crumbs, flour and baking powder.

2. In large bowl, beat EAGLE BRAND® and butter until smooth. Add crumb mixture; mix well. Stir in chocolate chips, coconut and walnuts. Drop by rounded tablespoonfuls onto ungreased baking sheets.

3. Bake 9 to 10 minutes or until lightly browned. Cool. Store leftovers loosely covered at room temperature.   *Makes about 3 dozen cookies*

Prep Time: 10 minutes
Bake Time: 9 to 10 minutes

chocolate peanut butter chip cookies

8 (1-ounce) squares semisweet chocolate
3 tablespoons butter or margarine
1 (14-ounce) can EAGLE BRAND® Sweetened Condensed Milk
    (NOT evaporated milk)
2 cups biscuit baking mix
1 egg
1 teaspoon vanilla extract
1 cup (6 ounces) peanut butter-flavored chips

1. Preheat oven to 350°F.

2. In large saucepan over low heat, melt chocolate and butter with EAGLE BRAND®; remove from heat. Add biscuit mix, egg and vanilla; with mixer, beat until smooth and well blended. Let mixture cool to room temperature. Stir in peanut butter chips. Drop by rounded teaspoonfuls onto ungreased baking sheets.

3. Bake 6 to 8 minutes or until tops are lightly crusted. Cool. Store leftovers tightly covered at room temperature.

Makes about 4 dozen cookies

Prep Time: 20 minutes
Bake Time: 6 to 8 minutes

fruit-packed
bars

holiday pumpkin treats

1³/₄ cups all-purpose flour
¹/₃ cup sugar
¹/₃ cup firmly packed light brown sugar
1 cup (2 sticks) cold butter or margarine
1 cup finely chopped nuts
1 (27-ounce) jar NONE SUCH® Ready-to-Use Mincemeat
   (Regular or Brandy & Rum)
1 (15-ounce) can pumpkin (2 cups)
1 (14-ounce) can EAGLE BRAND® Sweetened Condensed Milk
   (NOT evaporated milk)
2 eggs
1 teaspoon ground cinnamon
¹/₂ teaspoon ground allspice
¹/₂ teaspoon salt

1. Preheat oven to 425°F. Combine flour and sugars; cut in butter until crumbly. Stir in nuts. Reserve 1¹/₂ cups crumb mixture. Press remaining crumb mixture on bottom and halfway up sides of ungreased 13×9-inch baking pan. Spoon NONE SUCH® over crust.

2. Combine pumpkin, EAGLE BRAND®, eggs, cinnamon, allspice and salt; mix until smooth. Pour over NONE SUCH®. Top with reserved crumb mixture.

3. Bake 15 minutes. Reduce oven temperature to 350°F. Bake 40 minutes longer or until golden brown around edges. Cool. Cut into squares. Serve warm or at room temperature. Store leftovers covered in refrigerator.

Makes 1 to 2 dozen bars

Prep Time: 25 minutes
Bake Time: 55 minutes

brownie raspberry bars

1 cup (6 ounces) semisweet chocolate chips
¼ cup (½ stick) butter or margarine
2 cups biscuit baking mix
1 (14-ounce) can EAGLE BRAND® Sweetened Condensed Milk
    (NOT evaporated milk)
1 egg
1 teaspoon vanilla extract
1 cup chopped nuts
1 (8-ounce) package cream cheese, softened
½ cup powdered sugar
½ cup red raspberry jam
    Red food coloring (optional)
    Chocolate Drizzle (recipe follows)

1. Preheat oven to 350°F. In heavy saucepan, over low heat, melt chocolate chips with butter.

2. In large bowl, combine melted chocolate chips, biscuit mix, EAGLE BRAND®, egg and vanilla; mix well. Stir in nuts. Spread into well-greased 15×10-inch baking pan.

3. Bake 20 minutes or until center is set. Cool completely.

4. In small bowl beat cream cheese, sugar, jam and food coloring (optional) until smooth; spread over brownies. Garnish with Chocolate Drizzle. Chill. Cut into bars. Store covered in refrigerator.

Makes 3 to 4 dozen bars

Prep Time: 15 minutes
Bake Time: 20 minutes

chocolate drizzle: In heavy saucepan over low heat, melt ½ cup semisweet chocolate chips with 1 tablespoon shortening. Immediately drizzle over bars. Makes about ½ cup.

frozen lemon squares

1 1/4 cups graham cracker crumbs
1/4 cup sugar
1/4 cup (1/2 stick) butter or margarine, melted
3 egg yolks
1 (14-ounce) can EAGLE BRAND® Sweetened Condensed Milk
   (NOT evaporated milk)
1/2 cup lemon juice
   Yellow food coloring (optional)
   Whipped cream or non-dairy whipped topping

1. Preheat oven to 325°F. In small bowl, combine graham cracker crumbs, sugar and butter; press firmly on bottom of ungreased 8- or 9-inch square baking pan.

2. In small bowl, beat egg yolks, EAGLE BRAND®, lemon juice and food coloring (optional). Pour into prepared crust.

3. Bake 30 minutes. Cool completely. Top with whipped cream.

4. Freeze 4 hours or until firm. Let stand 10 minutes before serving. Garnish as desired. Store leftovers covered in freezer.

Makes 6 to 9 squares

Prep Time: 15 minutes
Bake Time: 30 minutes
Freeze Time: 4 hours

pumpkin cheesecake bars

> 1 (16-ounce) package pound cake mix
> 3 eggs, divided
> 2 tablespoons butter or margarine, melted
> 4 teaspoons pumpkin pie spice, divided
> 1 (8-ounce) package cream cheese, softened
> 1 (14-ounce) can EAGLE BRAND® Sweetened Condensed Milk
>   (NOT evaporated milk)
> 1 (15-ounce) can pumpkin (2 cups)
> ½ teaspoon salt
> 1 cup chopped nuts

1. Preheat oven to 350°F. In large bowl, combine cake mix, 1 egg, butter and 2 teaspoons pumpkin pie spice; beat on low speed until crumbly. Press onto bottom of ungreased 15×10-inch jellyroll pan.

2. In large bowl, beat cream cheese until fluffy. Gradually beat in EAGLE BRAND® until smooth. Beat in remaining 2 eggs, pumpkin, remaining 2 teaspoons pumpkin pie spice and salt; mix well.

3. Pour into prepared crust; sprinkle with nuts.

4. Bake 30 to 35 minutes or until set. Cool. Chill. Cut into bars. Store leftovers covered in refrigerator.   *Makes 4 dozen bars*

Prep Time: 10 minutes
Bake Time: 30 to 35 minutes

chocolate cranberry bars

2 cups vanilla wafer crumbs
$^{1}/_{2}$ cup unsweetened cocoa
3 tablespoons sugar
$^{2}/_{3}$ cup cold butter or margarine, cut into pieces
1 (14-ounce) can EAGLE BRAND® Sweetened Condensed Milk
  (NOT evaporated milk)
$1^{1}/_{3}$ cups (6-ounce package) sweetened dried cranberries or raisins
1 cup (6 ounces) peanut butter-flavored chips
1 cup finely chopped walnuts

1. Preheat oven to 350°F. In medium bowl, combine wafer crumbs, cocoa and sugar; cut in butter until crumbly. Press mixture evenly on bottom and $^{1}/_{2}$ inch up sides of ungreased 13×9-inch baking pan.

2. Pour EAGLE BRAND® evenly over crumb mixture. Sprinkle evenly with dried cranberries, peanut butter chips and walnuts; press down firmly.

3. Bake 25 to 30 minutes or until lightly browned. Cool completely in pan on wire rack. Cover with foil; let stand several hours. Cut into bars. Store covered at room temperature.   *Makes about 3 dozen bars*

Prep Time: 10 minutes
Bake Time: 25 to 30 minutes

strawberry swirl cheesecake bars

1 (10-ounce) package frozen strawberries, thawed (2½ cups)
1 tablespoon cornstarch
1¾ cups finely crushed cinnamon graham cracker crumbs
¼ cup (4 tablespoons) butter or margarine, melted
2 (8-ounce) packages cream cheese, softened
1 (14-ounce) can EAGLE BRAND® Sweetened Condensed Milk
   (NOT evaporated milk)
2 eggs
⅓ cup lemon juice
1 teaspoon vanilla extract

1. Preheat oven to 350°F. In blender container, blend strawberries until smooth. In saucepan over medium heat, combine strawberry purée and cornstarch; cook and stir until thickened. Cool.

2. In small bowl, combine graham cracker crumbs and butter; press firmly on bottom of greased 13×9-inch baking pan.

3. In large bowl, beat cream cheese until fluffy. Gradually beat in EAGLE BRAND® until smooth. Add eggs, lemon juice and vanilla; mix well. Pour over crust.

4. Drop strawberry mixture by spoonfuls over batter. Gently swirl with knife or spatula. Bake 25 to 30 minutes or until center is set. Cool. Chill. Cut into bars. Store leftovers covered in refrigerator.

Makes 2 to 3 dozen bars

Prep Time: 20 minutes
Bake Time: 25 to 30 minutes

To easily grease baking pans, place a small plastic food storage bag over one hand. Grab a small amount of butter or shortening with the covered hand and spread it evenly onto the sides and bottom of the pan. Then carefully remove the bag from your hand and discard it.

butterscotch apple squares

¼ cup (½ stick) butter or margarine
1½ cups graham cracker crumbs
2 small all-purpose apples, peeled and chopped (about 1¼ cups)
1 cup (6 ounces) butterscotch-flavored chips
1 (14-ounce) can EAGLE BRAND® Sweetened Condensed Milk
    (NOT evaporated milk)
1⅓ cups flaked coconut
1 cup chopped nuts

1. Preheat oven to 350°F (325°F for glass dish). In 13×9-inch baking pan, melt butter in oven. Sprinkle graham cracker crumbs evenly over butter; top with apples.

2. In heavy saucepan over medium heat, melt butterscotch chips with EAGLE BRAND®. Pour butterscotch mixture evenly over apples. Top with coconut and nuts; press down firmly.

3. Bake 25 to 30 minutes or until lightly browned. Cool. Cut into squares. Garnish as desired. Store leftovers covered in refrigerator.

Makes 1 dozen squares

Prep Time: 15 minutes
Bake Time: 25 to 30 minutes

lemon crumb bars

1 (18.25- or 18.5-ounce) package lemon or yellow cake mix
$^1\!/_2$ cup (1 stick) butter or margarine, softened
1 egg
2 cups finely crushed saltine crackers
1 (14-ounce) can EAGLE BRAND® Sweetened Condensed Milk
    (NOT evaporated milk)
$^1\!/_2$ cup lemon juice
3 egg yolks

1. Preheat oven to 350°F. In large bowl, combine cake mix, butter and 1 egg with mixer until crumbly. Stir in cracker crumbs. Reserve 2 cups crumb mixture. Press remaining crumb mixture firmly on bottom of greased 13×9-inch baking pan. Bake 15 to 20 minutes or until golden.

2. With mixer or wire whisk, beat EAGLE BRAND®, lemon juice and 3 egg yolks. Spread evenly over prepared crust. Top with reserved crumb mixture.

3. Bake 20 minutes longer or until set and top is golden. Cool. Cut into bars. Store leftovers covered in refrigerator.   *Makes 2 to 3 dozen bars*

Prep Time: 15 minutes
Bake Time: 35 to 40 minutes

harvest apple streusel squares

2 cups graham cracker crumbs
$^3/_4$ cup (1$^1/_2$ sticks) butter or margarine, melted
$^1/_2$ cup finely chopped pecans
1 (8-ounce) package cream cheese, softened
1 (14-ounce) can EAGLE BRAND® Sweetened Condensed Milk
   (NOT evaporated milk)
2 eggs
1 (21-ounce) can apple pie filling
$^1/_2$ cup firmly packed brown sugar
$^1/_2$ cup all-purpose flour
$^1/_4$ teaspoon ground cinnamon
$^1/_4$ cup ($^1/_2$ stick) cold butter or margarine
$^1/_2$ cup dried cranberries
$^1/_3$ cup chopped pecans

1. Preheat oven to 350°F. In small bowl, combine graham cracker crumbs, butter and finely chopped pecans. Press evenly into parchment paper-lined 13×9-inch baking pan.

2. In medium bowl, beat cream cheese until fluffy. Beat in EAGLE BRAND® until smooth. Add eggs; mix well. Pour over crust. Spoon apple pie filling over cream cheese layer.

3. In medium bowl, combine brown sugar, flour and cinnamon. Cut in cold butter until mixture resembles coarse crumbs. Stir in cranberries and chopped pecans. Sprinkle over apple layer. Bake 35 to 40 minutes or until golden (do not overbake). Cool. Cut into squares. Store leftovers covered in refrigerator.   *Makes 1 dozen squares*

Prep Time: 15 minutes
Bake Time: 35 to 40 minutes

lemony cheesecake bars

1½ cups graham cracker crumbs
⅓ cup sugar
⅓ cup finely chopped pecans
⅓ cup butter or margarine, melted
2 (8-ounce) packages cream cheese, softened
1 (14-ounce) can EAGLE BRAND® Sweetened Condensed Milk (NOT evaporated milk)
2 eggs
½ cup lemon juice

1. Preheat oven to 325°F. In medium bowl, combine graham cracker crumbs, sugar, pecans and butter. Reserve ⅓ cup crumb mixture; press remaining mixture firmly on bottom of ungreased 13×9-inch baking pan. Bake 6 minutes. Cool on wire rack.

2. In large bowl, beat cream cheese until fluffy. Gradually beat in EAGLE BRAND® until smooth. Add eggs and lemon juice; mix well. Carefully spoon mixture on top of crust. Spoon reserved crumb mixture to make diagonal stripes on top of cheese mixture or sprinkle to cover.

3. Bake about 30 minutes or until knife inserted near center comes out clean. Cool on wire rack 1 hour. Chill in refrigerator until serving time. Cut into bars to serve. Store leftovers covered in refrigerator.

Makes 2 dozen bars

Prep Time: 20 minutes
Bake Time: 36 minutes
Cool Time: 1 hour

pumpkin pie bars

1½ cups plus 1 tablespoon all-purpose flour, divided
1 cup finely chopped nuts
¾ cup (1½ sticks) butter or margarine
½ cup sugar
½ cup firmly packed brown sugar
2 teaspoons ground cinnamon, divided
1 (15-ounce) can pumpkin (2 cups)
1 (14-ounce) can EAGLE BRAND® Sweetened Condensed Milk
   (NOT evaporated milk)
2 eggs, beaten
½ teaspoon ground allspice
¼ teaspoon salt

1. Preheat oven to 375°F. In medium bowl, combine 1½ cups flour, nuts, butter, sugars and 1 teaspoon cinnamon. Add butter; mix until crumbly. Reserve 1¼ cups mixture. Press remaining mixture firmly on bottom of ungreased 13×9-inch baking pan.

2. In large bowl, combine pumpkin, EAGLE BRAND®, eggs, remaining 1 teaspoon cinnamon, allspice and salt; mix well. Pour evenly over crust.

3. Mix reserved crumbs with remaining 1 tablespoon flour. Sprinkle over pumpkin mixture. Bake 30 to 35 minutes or until set. Cool 10 minutes. Cut into bars. Serve warm. Store leftovers covered in refrigerator.

Makes 2 dozen bars

Prep Time: 15 minutes
Bake Time: 30 to 35 minutes

cranberry cheese squares

2 cups all-purpose flour
1½ cups oats
¾ cup plus 1 tablespoon firmly packed light brown sugar, divided
1 cup (2 sticks) butter or margarine, softened
1 (8-ounce) package cream cheese, softened
1 (14-ounce) can EAGLE BRAND® Sweetened Condensed Milk
    (NOT evaporated milk)
¼ cup lemon juice
2 tablespoons cornstarch
1 (16-ounce) can whole berry cranberry sauce

1. Preheat oven to 350°F. In large bowl, combine flour, oats, ¾ cup brown sugar and butter; mix until crumbly.

2. Reserve 1½ cups crumb mixture. Press remaining mixture firmly on bottom of greased 13×9-inch baking pan. Bake 15 minutes.

3. In medium bowl, beat cream cheese until fluffy. Gradually beat in EAGLE BRAND® until smooth; stir in lemon juice. Spread evenly over baked crust. In another medium bowl, combine cranberry sauce, cornstarch and remaining 1 tablespoon brown sugar. Spoon over cheese layer. Top with reserved crumb mixture.

4. Bake 40 minutes or until golden. Cool. Cut into squares. Store leftovers covered in refrigerator.   *Makes 2 to 3 dozen squares*

Prep Time: 20 minutes
Bake Time: 55 minutes

serving suggestion: Cut into larger squares. Serve warm and top with ice cream.

shaped cookies

easy peanut butter cookies

1 (14-ounce) can EAGLE BRAND® Sweetened Condensed Milk
   (NOT evaporated milk)
1 to 1¼ cups peanut butter
1 egg
1 teaspoon vanilla extract
2 cups biscuit baking mix
   Granulated sugar

1. In large bowl, beat EAGLE BRAND®, peanut butter, egg and vanilla until smooth. Add biscuit mix; mix well. Chill at least 1 hour.

2. Preheat oven to 350°F. Shape dough into 1-inch balls. Roll in sugar. Place 2 inches apart on ungreased baking sheets. Flatten with fork in criss-cross pattern.

3. Bake 6 to 8 minutes or until lightly browned (do not overbake). Cool. Store tightly covered at room temperature.

Makes about 5 dozen cookies

Prep Time: 10 minutes
Chill Time: 1 hour
Bake Time: 6 to 8 minutes

peanut blossom cookies: Make dough as directed above. Shape into 1-inch balls and roll in sugar; do not flatten. Bake as directed above. Immediately after baking, press solid milk chocolate candy kiss in center of each cookie.

peanut butter & jelly gems: Make dough as directed above. Shape into 1-inch balls and roll in sugar; do not flatten. Press thumb in center of each ball of dough; fill with jelly, jam or preserves. Proceed as directed above.

any-way-you-like 'em cookies: Stir 1 cup semisweet chocolate chips, chopped peanuts, raisins or flaked coconut into dough. Proceed as directed above.

cinnamon chip gems

1 cup (2 sticks) butter or margarine, softened
2 (3-ounce) packages cream cheese, softened
2 cups all-purpose flour
$\frac{1}{2}$ cup sugar
$\frac{1}{3}$ cup ground toasted almonds
2 eggs
1 (14-ounce) can EAGLE BRAND® Sweetened Condensed Milk
    (NOT evaporated milk)
1 teaspoon vanilla extract
1$\frac{1}{3}$ cups cinnamon baking chips, divided

1. In large bowl, beat butter and cream cheese until fluffy. Stir in flour, sugar and almonds. Cover; chill about 1 hour.

2. Divide dough into 4 equal parts. Shape each part into 12 smooth balls. Place each ball in ungreased small muffin cup (1$\frac{3}{4}$ inches in diameter); press evenly on bottom and up side of each cup.

3. Preheat oven to 375°F. In small bowl, beat eggs. Add EAGLE BRAND® and vanilla; mix well. Place 7 cinnamon baking chips in bottom of each muffin cup; generously fill three-fourths full with EAGLE BRAND® mixture.

4. Bake 18 to 20 minutes or until tops are puffed and just beginning to turn golden brown. Cool 3 minutes. Sprinkle about 10 chips on top of filling. Cool completely in pan on wire rack.

5. Remove from pan using small metal spatula or sharp knife. Cool completely. Store leftovers tightly covered at room temperature.

Makes 4 dozen gems

Prep Time: 20 minutes
Chill Time: 1 hour
Bake Time: 18 to 20 minutes

 For a pretty presentation, line the muffin pan with colorful paper baking cups before pressing the dough into the muffin pan cups.

banana split dessert pizza

1 (14-ounce) can EAGLE BRAND® Sweetened Condensed Milk
  (NOT evaporated milk)
½ cup sour cream
6 tablespoons lemon juice, divided
1 teaspoon vanilla extract
½ cup (1 stick) plus 1 tablespoon butter or margarine, softened
  and divided
¼ cup firmly packed brown sugar
1 cup all-purpose flour
¾ cup chopped nuts
3 medium bananas, sliced and divided
1 (8-ounce) can sliced pineapple, drained and cut in half
10 to 12 maraschino cherries drained and patted dry
  Additional chopped nuts for garnish
1 (1-ounce) square semisweet chocolate

1. Preheat oven to 375°F. In medium bowl, combine EAGLE BRAND®, sour cream, 4 tablespoons lemon juice and vanilla; mix well. Chill.

2. In large bowl, beat ½ cup (1 stick) butter and brown sugar until fluffy. Add flour and ¾ cup nuts; mix well.

3. On lightly greased pizza pan or baking sheet; press dough into 12-inch circle, forming rim around edge. Prick with fork. Bake 10 to 12 minutes or until golden brown. Cool.

4. Arrange 2 sliced bananas on cooled crust. Spoon filling evenly over bananas. Dip remaining banana slices in remaining 2 tablespoons lemon juice; arrange on top along with pineapple, cherries and additional nuts.

5. In small saucepan over low heat, melt chocolate with remaining 1 tablespoon butter; drizzle over pizza. Chill thoroughly. Store leftovers covered in refrigerator. *Makes one (12-inch) pizza*

Prep Time: 10 minutes
Bake Time: 10 to 12 minutes

peanut butter blossom cookies

1 (14-ounce) can EAGLE BRAND® Sweetened Condensed Milk
    (NOT evaporated milk)
¾ cup peanut butter
2 cups biscuit baking mix
1 teaspoon vanilla extract
⅓ cup sugar
65 solid milk chocolate candy kisses, unwrapped

1. Preheat oven to 375°F. In large bowl, beat EAGLE BRAND® and peanut butter until smooth. Add biscuit mix and vanilla; mix well.

2. Shape into 1-inch balls. Roll in sugar. Place 2 inches apart on ungreased baking sheets.

3. Bake 6 to 8 minutes or until lightly browned around edges (do not overbake). Remove from oven. Immediately press chocolate candy kiss in center of each cookie. Cool. Store leftovers tightly covered at room temperature.   *Makes about 5½ dozen cookies*

Prep Time: 25 minutes
Bake Time: 6 to 8 minutes

*Cookies and desserts made with EAGLE BRAND®
contain condensed all-natural milk. This gives your
family important bone-building calcium in every bite.*

petite macaroon cups

1 cup (2 sticks) butter or margarine, softened
2 (3-ounce) packages cream cheese, softened
2 cups all-purpose flour
1 (14-ounce) can EAGLE BRAND® Sweetened Condensed Milk
    (NOT evaporated milk)
2 eggs, beaten
1½ teaspoons vanilla extract
½ teaspoon almond extract
1⅓ cups flaked coconut

1. In large bowl, beat butter and cream cheese until fluffy; stir in flour. Cover; chill 1 hour.

2. Preheat oven to 375°F. Divide dough into quarters. On floured surface, shape 1 quarter into a smooth ball. Divide into 12 balls. Place each ball in ungreased small muffin cup (1¾ inches in diameter); press evenly on bottom and up side of each cup. Repeat with remaining dough.

3. In medium bowl, combine EAGLE BRAND®, eggs and extracts; mix well. Stir in coconut. Fill muffin cups three-fourths full.

4. Bake 16 to 18 minutes or until slightly browned. Cool in pans. Remove from pan using small metal spatula or knife. Store leftovers loosely covered at room temperature. *Makes 4 dozen cups*

chocolate macaroon cups: Beat ¼ cup unsweetened cocoa powder into egg mixture; proceed as above.

Prep Time: 25 minutes
Chill Time: 1 hour
Bake Time: 16 to 18 minutes

double chocolate cherry cookies

1¼ cups (2½ sticks) butter or margarine, softened
1¾ cups sugar
2 eggs
1 tablespoon vanilla extract
3½ cups all-purpose flour
¾ cup unsweetened cocoa powder
½ teaspoon baking powder
½ teaspoon baking soda
¼ teaspoon salt
2 (6-ounce) jars maraschino cherries (without stems), well
    drained and halved (about 72 cherry halves)
1 cup (6 ounces) semisweet chocolate chips
1 (14-ounce) can EAGLE BRAND® Sweetened Condensed Milk
    (NOT evaporated milk)

1. Preheat oven to 350°F. In large bowl, beat butter and sugar until fluffy; add eggs and vanilla; mix well.

2. In large bowl, combine flour, cocoa, baking powder, baking soda and salt; stir into butter mixture (dough will be stiff). Shape into 1-inch balls. Place 1 inch apart on ungreased baking sheets. Press cherry half into center of each cookie.

3. Bake 8 to 10 minutes. Cool.

4. In heavy saucepan over low heat, melt chocolate chips with EAGLE BRAND®; continue cooking about 3 minutes or until mixture thickens.

5. Frost each cookie, covering cherry. Store leftovers loosely covered at room temperature.   *Makes about 6 dozen cookies*

Prep Time: 15 minutes
Bake Time: 8 to 10 minutes

double chocolate pecan cookies: Prepare cookies as directed, omitting cherries; flatten. Bake as directed and frost tops. Garnish each cookie with pecan half.

cut-out cookies

3½ cups all-purpose flour
2 teaspoons baking powder
¼ teaspoon salt
1 (14-ounce) can EAGLE BRAND® Sweetened Condensed Milk
   (NOT evaporated milk)
¾ cup (1½ sticks) butter or margarine, softened
2 eggs
1 tablespoon vanilla extract
Colored sugar sprinkles (optional)
Powdered Sugar Glaze (optional, page 78)

1. In small bowl, combine flour, baking powder and salt; set aside.

2. In large bowl with mixer on low speed, beat EAGLE BRAND®, butter, eggs and vanilla just until blended. Beat on medium speed 1 minute or until smooth. Add flour mixture; beat on low speed until blended. (If using hand-held mixer, use wooden spoon to add last portion of flour mixture.)

3. Divide dough into thirds. Wrap and chill dough 2 hours or until easy to handle.

4. Preheat oven to 350°F. On lightly floured surface, roll out one portion of dough to ⅛-inch thickness. Cut out shapes with floured cookie cutters. Reroll as necessary to use all dough. Place cut-outs 1 inch apart on ungreased baking sheets. Sprinkle with colored sugar (optional).

5. Bake 9 to 11 minutes, or until very lightly browned around edges (do not overbake). Cool. Glaze and decorate (optional). Remove cookies to wire racks. Store leftovers loosely covered at room temperature. *Makes 5½ dozen cookies*

Prep Time: 15 minutes
Chill Time: 2 hours
Bake Time: 9 to 11 minutes

tip: Freeze Cut-Out Cookies in a tightly sealed container.

continued on page 78

powdered sugar glaze

   2 cups sifted powdered sugar
   ¹/₂ teaspoon vanilla extract
   2 tablespoons milk or whipping cream
   Food coloring (optional)

1. Whisk powdered sugar and vanilla, adding just enough milk or cream to bind into a glaze consistency. Add food coloring (optional) to tint glaze.   *Makes about 2 cups*

cookie pizza

   1 (18-ounce) package refrigerated sugar cookie dough
   2 cups (12 ounces) semisweet chocolate chips
   **1 (14-ounce) can EAGLE BRAND® Sweetened Condensed Milk
      (NOT evaporated milk)**
   2 cups candy-coated milk chocolate pieces
   2 cups miniature marshmallows
   ¹/₂ cup peanuts

1. Preheat oven to 375°F. Divide cookie dough in half; press into 2 ungreased 12-inch pizza pans. Bake 10 minutes or until golden. Remove from oven.

2. In medium saucepan over low heat, melt chocolate chips with EAGLE BRAND®. Spread over crusts. Sprinkle with chocolate pieces, marshmallows and peanuts.

3. Bake 4 minutes or until marshmallows are lightly toasted. Cool. Cut into wedges.   *Makes two (12-inch) pizzas*

Prep Time: 10 minutes
Bake Time: 14 minutes

nutty
bars

walnut caramel triangles

2 cups all-purpose flour
$\frac{1}{2}$ cup powdered sugar
1 cup (2 sticks) cold butter or margarine
1 (14-ounce) can EAGLE BRAND® Sweetened Condensed Milk
    (NOT evaporated milk)
$\frac{1}{2}$ cup whipping cream
1 teaspoon vanilla extract
1$\frac{1}{2}$ cups chopped walnuts
    Chocolate Drizzle (recipe follows)

1. Preheat oven to 350°F. In medium bowl, combine flour and powdered sugar; cut in butter until crumbly. Press firmly on bottom of ungreased 13×9-inch baking pan. Bake 15 minutes or until lightly browned around edges.

2. In heavy saucepan over medium-high heat, combine EAGLE BRAND®, whipping cream and vanilla. Cook and stir until mixture comes to a boil. Reduce heat to medium; cook and stir until mixture thickens, 8 to 10 minutes. Stir in walnuts. Spread evenly over crust.

3. Bake 20 minutes or until golden brown. Cool. Garnish with Chocolate Drizzle. Chill. Cut into triangles. Store leftovers covered at room temperature.   *Makes 4 dozen triangles*

Prep Time: 20 minutes
Bake Time: 35 minutes

chocolate drizzle: Melt $\frac{1}{2}$ cup semisweet chocolate chips with 1 teaspoon shortening. Carefully drizzle chocolate mixture over triangles with a spoon. Makes about $\frac{1}{2}$ cup.

brownie mint sundae squares

1 (19.5- or 22-ounce family size) package fudge brownie mix
³/₄ cup coarsely chopped walnuts
1 (14-ounce) can EAGLE BRAND® Sweetened Condensed Milk
    (NOT evaporated milk)
2 teaspoons peppermint extract
4 to 6 drops green food coloring (optional)
2 cups (1 pint) whipping cream, whipped
¹/₂ cup miniature semisweet chocolate chips
    Hot fudge sauce or chocolate-flavored syrup (optional)

1. Prepare brownie mix as package directs; stir in walnuts. Turn into foil-lined and greased 13×9-inch baking pan. Bake as directed. Cool completely.

2. In large bowl, combine EAGLE BRAND®, peppermint extract and food coloring (optional). Fold in whipped cream and chocolate chips. Spoon over brownie layer.

3. Cover; freeze 6 hours or until firm. To serve, lift brownies from pan with foil; cut into squares. Serve with hot fudge sauce (optional). Freeze leftovers. *Makes 10 to 12 servings*

Prep Time: 20 minutes
Freeze Time: 6 hours

Set baking pans on a cookie sheet to prevent the bottom of the brownies from becoming too hard. The cookie sheet will provide insulation from the oven heat. It will also keep the bottom of the brownies from cooking faster than the top.

golden peanut butter bars

2 cups all-purpose flour
¾ cup firmly packed light brown sugar
1 egg, beaten
½ cup (1 stick) cold butter or margarine
1 cup finely chopped peanuts
1 (14-ounce) can EAGLE BRAND® Sweetened Condensed Milk
  (NOT evaporated milk)
½ cup peanut butter
1 teaspoon vanilla extract

1. Preheat oven to 350°F. In large bowl, combine flour, brown sugar and egg; cut in butter until crumbly. Stir in peanuts. Reserve 2 cups crumb mixture. Press remaining mixture on bottom of ungreased 13×9-inch baking pan. Bake 15 minutes or until lightly browned.

2. In large bowl, beat EAGLE BRAND®, peanut butter and vanilla. Spread over crust; top with reserved crumb mixture.

3. Bake 25 minutes or until lightly browned. Cool. Chill if desired. Cut into bars. Store covered at room temperature.

Makes 2 to 3 dozen bars

Prep Time: 20 minutes
Bake Time: 40 minutes

double chocolate brownies

1¼ cups all-purpose flour, divided
¼ cup sugar
½ cup (1 stick) cold butter or margarine
1 (14-ounce) can EAGLE BRAND® Sweetened Condensed Milk
   (NOT evaporated milk)
¼ cup unsweetened cocoa
1 egg
1 teaspoon vanilla extract
½ teaspoon baking powder
1 (8-ounce) milk chocolate candy bar, broken into chunks
¾ cup chopped nuts

1. Preheat oven to 350°F.

2. In medium bowl, combine 1 cup flour and sugar; cut in butter until crumbly. Press firmly on bottom of foil-lined 13×9-inch baking pan. Bake 15 minutes.

3. In large bowl, beat EAGLE BRAND®, cocoa, egg, remaining ¼ cup flour, vanilla and baking powder. Stir in candy bar chunks and nuts. Spread over baked crust.

4. Bake 20 minutes or until set. Cool. Use foil to lift out of pan. Cut into bars. Store leftovers tightly covered at room temperature.

Makes 2 to 3 dozen brownies

Prep Time: 15 minutes
Bake Time: 35 minutes

Cutting brownies is easier if you place the entire pan in the freezer for 3 to 5 minutes. Run hot water over a sharp knife and wipe it dry. Cut the brownies with a back and forth sawing motion.

granola bars

> 3 cups oats
> 1 (14-ounce) can EAGLE BRAND® Sweetened Condensed Milk
>   (NOT evaporated milk)
> 1 cup peanuts
> 1 cup raisins
> 1 cup sunflower seeds
> ½ cup (1 stick) butter or margarine, melted
> 1½ teaspoons ground cinnamon

1. Preheat oven to 325°F.

2. In large bowl, combine oats, EAGLE BRAND®, peanuts, raisins, sunflower seeds, butter and cinnamon; mix well. Press evenly into foil-lined and greased 15×10-inch jellyroll pan.

3. Bake 25 to 30 minutes or until golden brown. Cool slightly; remove from pan and peel off foil. Cut into bars. Store loosely covered at room temperature.   *Makes 4 dozen bars*

Prep Time: 20 minutes
Bake Time: 25 to 30 minutes

chocolate almond bars

1½ cups all-purpose flour
⅔ cup sugar
¾ cup (1½ sticks) cold butter or margarine
1½ cups semisweet chocolate chips, divided
  1 (14-ounce) can EAGLE BRAND® Sweetened Condensed Milk
    (NOT evaporated milk)
  1 egg
  2 cups almonds, toasted and chopped
½ teaspoon almond extract
1 teaspoon solid shortening

1. Preheat oven to 350°F. In large bowl, combine flour and sugar; cut in butter until crumbly. Press firmly on bottom of ungreased 13×9-inch baking pan. Bake 20 minutes or until lightly browned.

2. In medium saucepan over low heat, melt 1 cup chocolate chips with EAGLE BRAND®. Remove from heat; cool slightly. Beat in egg. Stir in almonds and extract. Spread over baked crust.

3. Bake 25 minutes or until set. Cool.

4. Melt remaining ½ cup chocolate chips with shortening; drizzle over bars. Chill 10 minutes or until set. Cut into bars. Store covered at room temperature. *Makes 2 to 3 dozen bars*

Prep Time: 20 minutes
Bake Time: 45 minutes

pecan pie bars

2 cups all-purpose flour
$\frac{1}{4}$ cup firmly packed brown sugar
$\frac{1}{2}$ cup (1 stick) cold butter
$1\frac{1}{2}$ cups chopped pecans
1 (14-ounce) can EAGLE BRAND® Sweetened Condensed Milk
(NOT evaporated milk)
3 eggs, beaten
2 tablespoons lemon juice

1. Preheat oven to 350°F. In medium bowl, combine flour and brown sugar; cut in butter until crumbly.

2. Press mixture on bottom of ungreased 13×9-inch baking pan. Bake 10 to 15 minutes.

3. In large bowl, combine pecans, EAGLE BRAND®, eggs and lemon juice; pour over crust.

4. Bake 25 minutes or until filling is set. Cool. Chill if desired. Cut into bars. Store covered at room temperature.

Makes about 3 dozen bars

Prep Time: 15 minutes
Bake Time: 40 minutes

streusel caramel bars

    2 cups all-purpose flour
    ¾ cup firmly packed light brown sugar
    1 egg, beaten
    ¾ cup (1½ sticks) cold butter or margarine, divided
    ¾ cup chopped nuts
    24 caramels, unwrapped
    1 (14-ounce) can EAGLE BRAND® Sweetened Condensed Milk
        (NOT evaporated milk)

1. Preheat oven to 350°F. In large bowl, combine flour, brown sugar and egg; cut in ½ cup (1 stick) butter until crumbly. Stir in nuts.

2. Reserve 2 cups crumb mixture. Press remaining crumb mixture firmly on bottom of greased 13×9-inch baking pan. Bake 15 minutes.

3. In heavy saucepan over low heat, melt caramels and remaining ¼ cup (½ stick) butter with EAGLE BRAND®. Pour over crust. Top with reserved crumb mixture.

4. Bake 20 minutes or until bubbly. Cool. Chill if desired. Cut into bars. Store loosely covered at room temperature.

Makes 2 to 3 dozen bars

Prep Time: 25 minutes
Bake Time: 35 minutes

chocolate caramel bars: Melt 2 (1-ounce) squares unsweetened chocolate with caramels, EAGLE BRAND® and butter. Proceed as directed above.

chewy almond squares

1¼ cups graham cracker crumbs
¼ cup sugar
⅓ cup butter or margarine, melted
1 cup flaked coconut, toasted
1 cup chopped almonds, toasted*
1 (14-ounce) can EAGLE BRAND® Sweetened Condensed Milk
(NOT evaporated milk)

1 cup chopped pecans or walnuts, toasted, can be substituted.

1. Preheat oven to 375°F. In medium bowl, combine graham cracker crumbs, sugar and butter. Press firmly on bottom of foil-lined 9-inch square pan. Bake 5 to 7 minutes.

2. Sprinkle baked crust with coconut and almonds; pour EAGLE BRAND® evenly over top.

3. Bake 25 to 30 minutes. Cool on wire rack. Cut into squares. Store leftovers covered at room temperature.   *Makes 16 squares*

Prep Time: 10 minutes
Bake Time: 30 to 37 minutes

Table of Contents

.dreamy chocolate pies

decadent brownie pie

1 (9-inch) unbaked pie crust
1 cup (6 ounces) semisweet chocolate chips
¼ cup (½ stick) butter or margarine
1 (14-ounce) can EAGLE BRAND® Sweetened Condensed Milk
    (NOT evaporated milk)
½ cup biscuit baking mix
2 eggs
1 teaspoon vanilla extract
1 cup chopped nuts
    Vanilla ice cream (optional)

1. Preheat oven to 375°F. Bake pie crust 10 minutes; remove from oven. Reduce oven temperature to 325°F.

2. In small saucepan over low heat, melt chocolate chips with butter.

3. In large bowl, beat chocolate mixture, EAGLE BRAND®, biscuit mix, eggs and vanilla until smooth. Stir in nuts. Pour into baked crust.

4. Bake 40 to 45 minutes or until center is set. Cool at least 1 hour. Serve warm or at room temperature with ice cream (optional). Store leftovers covered in refrigerator.   *Makes one (9-inch) pie*

Prep Time: 20 minutes
Bake Time: 50 to 55 minutes
Cool Time: 1 hour

chocolate chiffon pie

2 (1-ounce) squares unsweetened chocolate, chopped
1 (14-ounce) can EAGLE BRAND® Sweetened Condensed Milk
    (NOT evaporated milk)
1 envelope unflavored gelatin
1/3 cup water
1/2 teaspoon vanilla extract
1 cup (1/2 pint) whipping cream, whipped
1 (6-ounce) prepared chocolate or graham cracker pie crust
    Additional whipped cream
    Shaved chocolate (optional)

1. In medium heavy saucepan over low heat, melt chocolate with EAGLE BRAND®.

2. In small saucepan, sprinkle gelatin over water; let stand 1 minute. Over low heat, stir until gelatin dissolves.

3. Combine chocolate mixture and gelatin. Add vanilla. Cool to room temperature. Fold in whipped cream. Spread into crust.

4. Chill 3 hours or until set. Garnish with additional whipped cream and shaved chocolate (optional). Store leftovers covered in refrigerator.

Makes one (6-ounce) pie

Prep Time: 20 minutes
Chill Time: 3 hours

fudgy pecan pie

$\frac{1}{4}$ cup ($\frac{1}{2}$ stick) butter or margarine
2 (1-ounce) squares unsweetened chocolate
1 (14-ounce) can EAGLE BRAND® Sweetened Condensed Milk
   (NOT evaporated milk)
$\frac{1}{2}$ cup hot water
2 eggs, well beaten
1$\frac{1}{4}$ cups pecan halves or pieces
1 teaspoon vanilla extract
$\frac{1}{8}$ teaspoon salt
1 (9-inch) unbaked pie crust

1. Preheat oven to 350°F.

2. In medium saucepan over low heat, melt butter and chocolate. Stir in EAGLE BRAND®, hot water and eggs; mix well. Remove from heat; stir in pecans, vanilla and salt. Pour into crust.

3. Bake 40 to 45 minutes or until center is set. Cool slightly. Serve warm or chilled. Garnish as desired. Store leftovers covered in refrigerator.

Makes one (9-inch) pie

Prep Time: 15 minutes
Bake Time: 40 to 45 minutes

chocolate truffle pie

1 envelope unflavored gelatin
$^1/_2$ cup water
3 (1-ounce) squares unsweetened or semisweet chocolate,
    melted and cooled
1 (14-ounce) can EAGLE BRAND® Sweetened Condensed Milk
    (NOT evaporated milk)
1 teaspoon vanilla extract
2 cups (1 pint) whipping cream, whipped
1 (6-ounce) prepared chocolate crumb pie crust

1. In small saucepan, sprinkle gelatin over water; let stand 1 minute. Over low heat, stir until gelatin dissolves.

2. In large bowl, beat chocolate with EAGLE BRAND® until smooth. Stir in gelatin mixture and vanilla. Fold in whipped cream. Pour into crust.

3. Chill 3 hours or until set. Garnish as desired. Store leftovers covered in refrigerator. *Makes one (6-ounce) pie*

Prep Time: 15 minutes
Chill Time: 3 hours

 Before beating whipping cream, make sure the cream, bowl and beaters are chilled. The cold will keep the fat in the cream solid, therefore increasing the volume.

chocolate-peanut butter mousse pie

1 cup chocolate graham cracker crumbs
$^1/_3$ cup honey-roasted peanuts, finely chopped
6 tablespoons butter or margarine, softened
1$^1/_2$ cups whipping cream, divided
1 (14-ounce) can EAGLE BRAND® Sweetened Condensed Milk
 (NOT evaporated milk), divided
1$^1/_2$ cups semisweet chocolate chips
2 (3-ounce) packages cream cheese, softened
$^3/_4$ cup creamy peanut butter

Microwave Directions

1. In medium bowl, combine graham cracker crumbs, peanuts and butter. Press mixture on bottom and up side of ungreased 9-inch pie plate. Set aside.

2. Pour $^1/_2$ cup whipping cream into microwave-safe bowl; microwave on HIGH (100% power) 2 minutes. Stir in $^1/_2$ cup EAGLE BRAND® and chocolate chips until smooth. Pour into crust. Chill 1 hour.

3. In large bowl, beat remaining whipping cream until stiff peaks form; set aside. In small bowl, beat remaining EAGLE BRAND®, cream cheese and peanut butter until smooth. Fold in whipped cream. Spoon over chocolate filling.

4. Freeze 4 to 6 hours or until firm. Let stand 15 minutes before serving. Garnish as desired. Store leftovers covered in freezer.

Makes one (9-inch) pie

Prep Time: 20 minutes
Chill Time: 1 hour
Freeze Time: 4 to 6 hours

heavenly chocolate mousse pie

4 (1-ounce) squares unsweetened chocolate, melted
1 (14-ounce) can EAGLE BRAND® Sweetened Condensed Milk
    (NOT evaporated milk)
1½ teaspoons vanilla extract
1 cup (½ pint) whipping cream, whipped
1 (6-ounce) prepared chocolate crumb pie crust

1. In large bowl, beat chocolate with EAGLE BRAND® and vanilla until well blended.

2. Chill 15 minutes or until cool; stir until smooth. Fold in whipped cream. Pour into crust.

3. Chill thoroughly. Garnish as desired. Store leftovers covered in refrigerator.   *Makes one (6-ounce) pie*

Prep Time: 20 minutes

Unsweetened chocolate is also known as baking or bitter chocolate. It is pure chocolate; no flavorings or sugar have been added.

chocolate pie

1 (14-ounce) can EAGLE BRAND® Sweetened Condensed Milk
   (NOT evaporated milk)
2 (1-ounce) squares unsweetened chocolate
¼ teaspoon salt
¼ cup hot water
½ teaspoon vanilla extract
1 cup whipping cream, whipped
1 (9-inch) baked pie crust, cooled
   Additional whipped cream, shaved chocolate or chopped nuts
   (optional)

1. In top of double boiler, combine EAGLE BRAND®, chocolate and salt. Cook over hot water, stirring constantly, until mixture is very thick. Gradually add water, stirring constantly to keep mixture smooth. Continue to cook and stir 2 to 5 minutes, or until mixture thickens again. Remove from heat. Stir in vanilla.

2. Chill mixture in refrigerator until cool; fold in whipped cream. Pour into baked crust. Refrigerate 4 hours.

3. Garnish with additional whipped cream, shaved chocolate or chopped nuts (optional). Store leftovers covered in refrigerator.

Makes one (9-inch) pie

Prep Time: 15 minutes

rich & creamy cheesecakes

brownie chocolate chip cheesecake

1 (19.5- or 22-ounce) package fudge brownie mix
3 (8-ounce) packages cream cheese, softened
1 (14-ounce) can EAGLE BRAND® Sweetened Condensed Milk
    (NOT evaporated milk)
3 eggs
2 teaspoons vanilla extract
$\frac{1}{2}$ cup miniature semisweet chocolate chips

1. Preheat oven to 350°F. Grease bottom only of 9-inch springform pan. Prepare brownie mix as package directs for chewy brownies. Spread evenly in prepared pan. Bake 35 minutes or until set. Reduce oven temperature to 300°F.

2. In large bowl, beat cream cheese until fluffy. Gradually beat in EAGLE BRAND® until smooth. Add eggs and vanilla; mix well. Stir in chocolate chips. Pour into baked crust.

3. Reduce oven temperature to 300°F. Bake 50 minutes or until set. Cool. Chill thoroughly. Remove side of springform pan. Garnish as desired. Store leftovers covered in refrigerator.

Makes one (9-inch) cheesecake

Prep Time: 20 minutes
Bake Time: 1 hour 25 minutes

note: Chocolate chips may fall to brownie layer during baking.

mini cheesecakes

1½ cups graham cracker or chocolate wafer cookie crumbs
¼ cup sugar
¼ cup (½ stick) butter or margarine, melted
3 (8-ounce) packages cream cheese, softened
1 (14-ounce) can EAGLE BRAND® Sweetened Condensed Milk (NOT evaporated milk)
3 eggs
2 teaspoons vanilla extract

1. Preheat oven to 300°F. In small bowl, combine graham cracker crumbs, sugar and butter; press equal portions firmly on bottoms of 24 lightly greased or foil-lined muffin cups.

2. In large bowl, beat cream cheese until fluffy. Gradually beat in EAGLE BRAND® until smooth. Add eggs and vanilla; mix well. Spoon equal amounts of mixture (about 3 tablespoons) into crusts.

3. Bake 20 minutes or until cheesecakes spring back when lightly touched. Cool.* Chill. Garnish as desired. Store leftovers covered in refrigerator. *Makes 2 dozen mini cheesecakes*

If greased muffin cups are used, cool baked cheesecakes. Freeze 15 minutes; remove with narrow spatula. Proceed as directed above.

Prep Time: 20 minutes
Bake Time: 20 minutes

chocolate mini cheesecakes: Melt 1 cup (6 ounces) semisweet chocolate chips; mix into batter. Proceed as directed above, baking 20 to 25 minutes.

maple pumpkin cheesecake

1¼ cups graham cracker crumbs
¼ cup sugar
¼ cup (½ stick) butter or margarine, melted
3 (8-ounce) packages cream cheese, softened
1 (14-ounce) can EAGLE BRAND® Sweetened Condensed Milk
  (NOT evaporated milk)
1 (15-ounce) can pumpkin (2 cups)
3 eggs
¼ cup pure maple syrup
1½ teaspoons ground cinnamon
1 teaspoon ground nutmeg
½ teaspoon salt
  Maple Pecan Glaze (recipe follows)

1. Preheat oven to 325°F. Combine graham cracker crumbs, sugar and butter; press firmly on bottom of ungreased 9-inch springform pan.

2. In large bowl, beat cream cheese until fluffy. Gradually beat in EAGLE BRAND® until smooth. Add pumpkin, eggs, maple syrup, cinnamon, nutmeg and salt; mix well. Pour into crust.

3. Bake 1 hour 15 minutes or until center appears nearly set when shaken. Cool 1 hour. Cover and chill at least 4 hours. Top with chilled Maple Pecan Glaze. Store leftovers covered in refrigerator.

Makes one (9-inch) cheesecake

Prep Time: 25 minutes
Bake Time: 1 hour and 15 minutes
Cool Time: 1 hour
Chill Time: 4 hours

maple pecan glaze: In medium saucepan over medium-high heat, combine 1 cup (½ pint) whipping cream and ¾ cup pure maple syrup; bring to a boil. Boil rapidly 15 to 20 minutes or until thickened, stirring occasionally. Add ½ cup chopped pecans. Cover and chill. Stir before using. Makes about 2½ cups.

apple cinnamon cheesecake

1/2 cup (1 stick) plus 1 tablespoon butter or margarine, softened
    and divided
1/4 cup firmly packed light brown sugar
1 cup all-purpose flour
1/4 cup quick-cooking oats
1/4 cup finely chopped walnuts
1/2 teaspoon ground cinnamon
2 (8-ounce) packages cream cheese, softened
1 (14-ounce) can EAGLE BRAND® Sweetened Condensed Milk
    (NOT evaporated milk)
3 eggs
1/2 cup frozen apple juice concentrate, thawed
2 medium apples, cored and sliced
    Cinnamon Apple Glaze (recipe follows)

1. Preheat oven to 300°F. In small bowl, beat 1/2 cup (1 stick) butter and brown sugar until fluffy. Add flour, oats, walnuts and cinnamon; mix well. Press firmly on bottom and halfway up side of ungreased 9-inch springform pan. Bake 10 minutes.

2. In large bowl, beat cream cheese until fluffy. Gradually beat in EAGLE BRAND® until smooth. Add eggs and apple juice concentrate; mix well. Pour into baked crust.

3. Bake 45 minutes or until center springs back when lightly touched. Cool.

4. In large skillet, cook apples in remaining 1 tablespoon butter until tender-crisp. Arrange on top of cheesecake; drizzle with Cinnamon Apple Glaze. Chill. Store leftovers covered in refrigerator.

Makes one (9-inch) cheesecake

cinnamon apple glaze

1/4 cup frozen apple juice concentrate, thawed
1 teaspoon cornstarch
1/4 teaspoon ground cinnamon

1. In small saucepan, combine juice concentrate, cornstarch and cinnamon; mix well. Over low heat, cook and stir until thickened.

Makes about 1/2 cup

almond praline cheesecake

¾ cup graham cracker crumbs
½ cup slivered almonds, toasted and finely chopped
¼ cup firmly packed brown sugar
¼ cup (½ stick) butter or margarine, melted
3 (8-ounce) packages cream cheese, softened
1 (14-ounce) can EAGLE BRAND® Sweetened Condensed Milk
    (NOT evaporated milk)
3 eggs
1 teaspoon almond extract
Almond Praline Topping (recipe follows)

1. Preheat oven to 300°F. In medium bowl, combine graham cracker crumbs, almonds, brown sugar and butter; press on bottom of ungreased 9-inch springform pan or 13×9-inch baking pan.

2. In large bowl, beat cream cheese until fluffy. Gradually beat in EAGLE BRAND® until smooth. Add eggs and almond extract; mix well. Pour into crust.

3. Bake 55 to 60 minutes or until center is set. Cool. Top with Almond Praline Topping. Chill. Store leftovers covered in refrigerator.

Makes one (9-inch or 13×9-inch) cheesecake

Prep Time: 15 minutes
Bake Time: 55 to 60 minutes

almond praline topping

⅓ cup firmly packed dark brown sugar
⅓ cup whipping cream
½ cup slivered almonds, toasted and finely chopped

1. In small saucepan over medium heat, combine brown sugar and whipping cream. Cook and stir until sugar dissolves. Simmer 5 minutes or until thickened. Remove from heat; add almonds.

2. Spoon evenly over cheesecake. (To make topping for 13×9-inch baking pan, double all topping ingredients; simmer 10 to 12 minutes or until thickened.)

Makes about 1 cup

black & white cheesecake

2 (3-ounce) packages cream cheese, softened
1 (14-ounce) can EAGLE BRAND® Sweetened Condensed Milk
   (NOT evaporated milk)
1 egg
1 teaspoon vanilla extract
1/2 cup miniature semisweet chocolate chips
1 teaspoon all-purpose flour
1 (6-ounce) prepared chocolate crumb pie crust
   Chocolate Glaze (recipe follows)

1. Preheat oven to 350°F.

2. In medium bowl, beat cream cheese until fluffy. Gradually beat in EAGLE BRAND® until smooth. Add egg and vanilla; mix well.

3. In small bowl, toss chocolate chips with flour to coat; stir into cream cheese mixture. Pour into crust.

4. Bake 35 minutes or until center springs back when lightly touched. Cool. Prepare Chocolate Glaze and spread over cheesecake. Chill. Store leftovers covered in refrigerator.

Makes one (6-ounce) cheesecake

Prep Time: 15 minutes
Bake Time: 35 minutes

chocolate glaze: In small saucepan over low heat, melt 1/2 cup miniature semisweet chocolate chips with 1/4 cup whipping cream. Cook and stir until thickened and smooth. Use immediately. Makes about 1 cup.

raspberry swirl cheesecakes

1½ cups fresh or frozen red raspberries, thawed
1 (14-ounce) can EAGLE BRAND® Sweetened Condensed Milk
    (NOT evaporated milk), divided
2 (8-ounce) packages cream cheese, softened
3 eggs
2 (6-ounce) prepared chocolate crumb pie crusts
    Chocolate and white chocolate leaves (optional)
    Fresh raspberries for garnish (optional)

1. Preheat oven to 350°F. In blender container, blend 1½ cups raspberries until smooth; press through sieve to remove seeds. Stir ⅓ cup EAGLE BRAND® into raspberry purée; set aside.

2. In large bowl, beat cream cheese until fluffy. Gradually beat in remaining EAGLE BRAND® until smooth. Add eggs, mix well. Spoon into crusts. Drizzle with raspberry mixture. With knife, gently swirl raspberry mixture through cream cheese mixture.

3. Bake 25 minutes or until centers are nearly set when shaken. Cool. Cover and chill at least 4 hours. Garnish with chocolate leaves and fresh raspberries (optional). Store leftovers covered in refrigerator.

Makes two (6-ounce) cheesecakes

Prep Time: 15 minutes
Bake Time: 25 minutes
Chill Time: 4 hours

chocolate leaves: Place 1 (1-ounce) square semisweet or white chocolate in microwave-safe bowl. Microwave on HIGH (100% power) 1 to 2 minutes, stirring every minute until smooth. With small, clean paintbrush, paint several coats of melted chocolate on undersides of nontoxic leaves, such as mint, lemon or strawberry. Wipe off any chocolate from top sides of leaves. Place leaves, chocolate sides up, on wax paper-lined baking sheet or on curved surface, such as rolling pin. Refrigerate leaves until chocolate is firm. To use, carefully peel leaves away from chocolate. Makes about 2 dozen.

triple chocolate cheesecakes

1 envelope unflavored gelatin
½ cup cold water
2 (8-ounce) packages cream cheese, softened
1 (14-ounce) can EAGLE BRAND® Sweetened Condensed Milk
   (NOT evaporated milk)
4 (1-ounce) squares unsweetened chocolate, melted and slightly
   cooled
1 (8-ounce) container frozen non-dairy whipped topping, thawed
½ cup miniature semisweet chocolate chips
1 (21-ounce) can cherry pie filling (optional)
2 (6-ounce) prepared chocolate crumb pie crusts

1. In 1-cup glass measure, combine gelatin and cold water; let stand 5 minutes to soften. Pour about 1 inch water into small saucepan; place glass measure in saucepan. Place saucepan over medium heat; stir until gelatin is dissolved. Remove measure from saucepan; cool slightly.

2. In large bowl, beat cream cheese until fluffy. Gradually beat in EAGLE BRAND® and melted chocolate until smooth. Gradually beat in gelatin mixture. Fold in whipped topping and chocolate chips. Spread pie filling on bottoms of crusts (optional). Pour chocolate mixture into crusts.

3. Cover and chill at least 4 hours. Store leftovers covered in refrigerator.   *Makes two (6-ounce) cheesecakes*

Prep Time: 20 minutes
Chill Time: 4 hours

To store these cheesecakes in the freezer, cover and freeze them for up to 1 month. Serve the cheesecakes frozen, or remove them from the freezer several hours before serving and let them thaw in the refrigerator.

creamy baked cheesecake

1¼ cups graham cracker crumbs
⅓ cup butter or margarine, melted
¼ cup sugar
2 (8-ounce) packages cream cheese, softened
1 (14-ounce) can EAGLE BRAND® Sweetened Condensed Milk
 (NOT evaporated milk)
3 eggs
¼ cup lemon juice
1 (8-ounce) container sour cream, at room temperature
Raspberry Topping (recipe follows, optional)

1. Preheat oven to 300°F. In small bowl, combine graham cracker crumbs, butter and sugar; press firmly on bottom of ungreased 9-inch springform pan.

2. In large bowl, beat cream cheese until fluffy. Gradually beat in EAGLE BRAND® until smooth. Add eggs and lemon juice; mix well. Pour into crust.

3. Bake 50 to 55 minutes or until set. Remove from oven; top with sour cream. Bake 5 minutes longer. Cool. Chill. Prepare Raspberry Topping (optional) and serve with cheesecake. Store leftovers covered in refrigerator. *Makes one (9-inch) cheesecake*

Prep Time: 25 minutes
Bake Time: 55 to 60 minutes
Chill Time: 4 hours

raspberry topping

2 cups water
½ cup powdered sugar
¼ cup red raspberry jam
1 tablespoon cornstarch
1 cup frozen red raspberries

1. In small saucepan over medium heat, combine water, powdered sugar, jam and cornstarch. Cook and stir until thickened and clear. Cool. Stir in raspberries. *Makes about 3½ cups*

luscious baked chocolate cheesecake

1¼ cups graham cracker crumbs
⅓ cup butter or margarine, melted
¼ cup sugar
3 (8-ounce) packages cream cheese, softened
1 (14-ounce) can EAGLE BRAND® Sweetened Condensed Milk
   (NOT evaporated milk)
2 cups (12-ounces) semisweet chocolate chips *or* 8 (1-ounce)
   squares semisweet chocolate, melted
4 eggs
2 teaspoons vanilla extract

1. Preheat oven to 300°F. Combine graham cracker crumbs, butter and sugar; press firmly on bottom of ungreased 9-inch springform pan.

2. In large bowl, beat cream cheese until fluffy. Gradually beat in EAGLE BRAND® until smooth. Add chocolate chips, eggs and vanilla; mix well. Pour into crust.

3. Bake 65 minutes or until center is set. Cool to room temperature. Chill. Garnish as desired. Store leftovers covered in refrigerator.

Makes one (9-inch) cheesecake

Prep Time: 20 minutes
Bake Time: 65 minutes

 To avoid messy oven cleanup, place a baking sheet under the springform pan to catch any drips.

chocolate raspberry cheesecake

2 (3-ounce) packages cream cheese, softened
1 (14-ounce) can EAGLE BRAND® Sweetened Condensed Milk
   (NOT evaporated milk)
1 egg
3 tablespoons lemon juice
1 teaspoon vanilla extract
1 cup fresh or frozen raspberries
1 (6-ounce) prepared chocolate crumb pie crust
   Chocolate Glaze (recipe follows)

1. Preheat oven to 350°F.

2. In medium bowl, beat cream cheese until fluffy. Gradually beat in
EAGLE BRAND® until smooth. Add egg, lemon juice and vanilla; mix
well. Arrange raspberries on bottom of crust. Slowly pour cheese
mixture over fruit.

3. Bake 30 to 35 minutes or until center is almost set. Cool.

4. Prepare Chocolate Glaze and spread over cheesecake; chill. Garnish
as desired. Store leftovers covered in refrigerator.

Makes one (6-ounce) cheesecake

Prep Time: 20 minutes
Bake Time: 30 to 35 minutes

chocolate glaze: In small saucepan over low heat, melt 2 (1-ounce)
squares semisweet chocolate with ¼ cup whipping cream. Cook and
stir until thickened and smooth. Remove from heat; cool slightly.
Makes about ½ cup.

black forest chocolate cheesecake

1½ cups chocolate cookie crumbs
3 tablespoons butter or margarine, melted
2 (1-ounce) squares unsweetened chocolate
1 (14-ounce) can EAGLE BRAND® Sweetened Condensed Milk
   (NOT evaporated milk)
2 (8-ounce) packages cream cheese, softened
3 eggs
3 tablespoons cornstarch
1 teaspoon almond extract
1 (21-ounce) can cherry pie filling, chilled

1. Preheat oven to 300°F. In small bowl, combine cookie crumbs and butter; press firmly on bottom of ungreased 9-inch springform pan.

2. In small saucepan over low heat, melt chocolate with EAGLE BRAND®, stirring constantly. Remove from heat.

3. In large bowl, beat cream cheese until fluffy. Gradually beat in EAGLE BRAND® mixture until smooth. Add eggs, cornstarch and almond extract; mix well. Pour into crust.

4. Bake 50 to 55 minutes or until center is set. Cool and chill overnight. Top with cherry pie filling before serving. Store leftovers covered in refrigerator.   *Makes one (9-inch) cheesecake*

Prep Time: 20 minutes
Bake Time: 50 to 55 minutes

chocolate chip cheesecake

1½ cups finely crushed crème-filled chocolate sandwich cookie
    crumbs (about 18 cookies)
2 to 3 tablespoons butter or margarine, melted
3 (8-ounce) packages cream cheese, softened
1 (14-ounce) can EAGLE BRAND® Sweetened Condensed Milk
    (NOT evaporated milk)
3 eggs
2 teaspoons vanilla extract
1 cup (6 ounces) miniature semisweet chocolate chips, divided
1 teaspoon all-purpose flour

1. Preheat oven to 300°F. In small bowl, combine cookie crumbs and butter; press firmly on bottom of ungreased 9-inch springform pan.

2. In large bowl, beat cream cheese until fluffy. Gradually beat in EAGLE BRAND® until smooth. Add eggs and vanilla; mix well.

3. In small bowl, toss ½ cup chocolate chips with flour to coat; stir into cheese mixture. Pour into crust. Sprinkle remaining ½ cup chocolate chips evenly over top.

4. Bake 55 to 60 minutes or until set. Cool. Chill. Garnish as desired. Store leftovers covered in refrigerator.

Makes one (9-inch) cheesecake

Prep Time: 15 minutes
Bake Time: 55 to 60 minutes

For the best distribution of the chocolate chips throughout this cheesecake, do not oversoften or overbeat the cream cheese.

.decadent
pies

fluffy peanut butter pie

 ¼ cup (½ stick) butter or margarine
 2 cups finely crushed crème-filled chocolate sandwich cookies
   (about 20 cookies)
 1 (8-ounce) package cream cheese, softened
 1 (14-ounce) can EAGLE BRAND® Sweetened Condensed Milk
   (NOT evaporated milk)
 1 cup smooth or crunchy peanut butter
 3 tablespoons lemon juice
 1 teaspoon vanilla extract
 1 cup (½ pint) whipping cream, whipped

1. In small saucepan over low heat, melt butter; stir in cookie crumbs. Press crumb mixture firmly on bottom and up side of 9-inch pie plate; chill while preparing filling.

2. In large bowl, beat cream cheese until fluffy. Gradually add EAGLE BRAND® and peanut butter until smooth. Add lemon juice and vanilla; mix well. Fold in whipped cream. Pour into crust.

3. Chill 4 hours or until set. Garnish as desired. Store leftovers covered in refrigerator.   *Makes one (9-inch) pie*

Prep Time: 20 minutes
Chill Time: 4 hours

sweet potato pecan pie

    1 pound sweet potatoes or yams, cooked and peeled
   ¼ cup (½ stick) butter or margarine, softened
    1 (14-ounce) can EAGLE BRAND® Sweetened Condensed Milk
       (NOT evaporated milk)
    1 egg
    1 teaspoon freshly grated orange rind
    1 teaspoon ground cinnamon
    1 teaspoon vanilla extract
   ½ teaspoon ground nutmeg
   ¼ teaspoon salt
    1 (6-ounce) prepared graham cracker pie crust
    Pecan Topping (recipe follows)

1. Preheat oven to 425°F.

2. In large bowl, beat hot sweet potatoes and butter until smooth. Add EAGLE BRAND®, egg, orange rind, cinnamon, vanilla, nutmeg and salt; mix well. Pour into crust. Bake 20 minutes.

3. Meanwhile, prepare Pecan Topping.

4. Remove pie from oven; reduce oven temperature to 350°F. Spoon Pecan Topping over pie.

5. Bake 25 minutes longer or until set. Cool. Serve warm or at room temperature. Store leftovers covered in refrigerator.

Makes one (6-ounce) pie

Prep Time: 30 minutes
Bake Time: 45 minutes

pecan topping: In small bowl, beat 1 egg, 2 tablespoons firmly packed light brown sugar, 2 tablespoons dark corn syrup, 1 tablespoon melted butter and ½ teaspoon maple flavoring. Stir in 1 cup chopped pecans. Makes about 2 cups.

traditional peanut butter pie

⅓ cup creamy peanut butter
¾ cup powdered sugar
1 (9-inch) baked pie crust
1 (14-ounce) can EAGLE BRAND® Sweetened Condensed Milk
    (NOT evaporated milk)
4 eggs, separated
½ cup water
1 (4-serving size) package cook-and-serve vanilla pudding mix
1 (8-ounce) container sour cream, at room temperature
¼ teaspoon cream of tartar
6 tablespoons granulated sugar

1. Preheat oven to 350°F. In small bowl, cut peanut butter into powdered sugar until crumbly; sprinkle into crust.

2. In large saucepan over medium heat, combine EAGLE BRAND®, egg yolks, water and pudding mix; cook and stir until thickened. Cool slightly; stir in sour cream. Pour into crust.

3. In small bowl, beat egg whites and cream of tartar with electric mixer on high speed until soft peaks form. Gradually beat in sugar, 1 tablespoon at a time; beat 4 minutes longer or until sugar is dissolved and stiff, glossy peaks form.

4. Spread meringue over pie, carefully sealing to edge of crust to prevent meringue from shrinking. Bake 15 minutes or until golden. Cool 1 hour. Chill at least 3 hours. Store leftovers covered in refrigerator.

Makes one (9-inch) pie

Prep Time: 30 minutes
Bake Time: 15 minutes
Cool Time: 1 hour
Chill Time: 3 hours

sweet potato pie

1 pound sweet potatoes,* boiled and peeled
¼ cup (½ stick) butter or margarine
1 (14-ounce) can EAGLE BRAND® Sweetened Condensed Milk
    (NOT evaporated milk)
2 eggs
1 teaspoon grated orange rind
1 teaspoon vanilla extract
1 teaspoon ground cinnamon
1 teaspoon ground nutmeg
¼ teaspoon salt
1 (9-inch) unbaked pie crust

*For best results, use fresh sweet potatoes.

1. Preheat oven to 350°F.

2. In large bowl, beat sweet potatoes and butter until smooth. Add EAGLE BRAND®, eggs, orange rind, vanilla, cinnamon, nutmeg and salt; mix well. Pour into crust.

3. Bake 40 minutes or until golden brown. Cool. Garnish as desired. Store leftovers covered in refrigerator.   *Makes one (9-inch) pie*

Prep Time: 20 minutes
Bake Time: 40 minutes

peanut butter pie

Chocolate Crunch Crust (recipe follows)
1 (8-ounce) package cream cheese, softened
1 (14-ounce) can EAGLE BRAND® Sweetened Condensed Milk
(NOT evaporated milk)
³/₄ cup creamy peanut butter
2 tablespoons lemon juice
1 teaspoon vanilla extract
1 cup whipping cream, whipped *or* 1 (4-ounce) container frozen
non-dairy whipped topping, thawed
Chocolate fudge ice cream topping

1. Prepare Chocolate Crunch Crust.

2. In large bowl, beat cream cheese until fluffy. Gradually beat in EAGLE BRAND® and peanut butter until smooth. Add lemon juice and vanilla; mix well. Fold in whipped cream. Spread into baked crust.

3. Drizzle topping over pie. Refrigerate 4 to 5 hours or until firm. Store leftovers covered in refrigerator.   *Makes one (9-inch) pie*

Prep Time: 20 minutes
Chill Time: 4 to 5 hours

chocolate crunch crust: In heavy saucepan over low heat, melt ¹/₃ cup butter or margarine and 1 (6-ounce) package semisweet chocolate chips. Remove from heat; gently stir in 2¹/₂ cups oven-toasted rice cereal until completely coated. Press on bottom and up side to rim of buttered 9-inch pie plate. Chill 30 minutes.

cakes .&
frostings

apple spice custard cake

1 (18.25- or 18.5-ounce) package spice cake mix
2 medium apples, peeled, cored and chopped
1 (14-ounce) can EAGLE BRAND® Sweetened Condensed Milk
    (NOT evaporated milk)
1 (8-ounce) container sour cream
¼ cup lemon juice
    Ground cinnamon (optional)

1. Preheat oven to 350°F.

2. Prepare cake mix according to package directions. Stir in apples. Pour batter into greased and floured 13×9-inch baking pan. Bake 30 to 35 minutes or until toothpick inserted near center comes out clean.

3. In medium bowl, combine EAGLE BRAND® and sour cream; mix well. Stir in lemon juice. Remove cake from oven; spread sour cream mixture evenly over hot cake.

4. Return to oven; bake 5 minutes or until set. Sprinkle with cinnamon (optional). Cool. Chill. Store leftovers covered in refrigerator.

Makes one (13×9-inch) cake

Prep Time: 15 minutes
Bake Time: 35 to 40 minutes

coconut lemon torte

1 (14-ounce) can EAGLE BRAND® Sweetened Condensed Milk
  (NOT evaporated milk)
2 egg yolks
½ cup lemon juice
1 teaspoon grated lemon rind (optional)
  Yellow food coloring (optional)
1 (18.25- or 18.5-ounce) package white cake mix
1 (4-ounce) container frozen nondairy whipped topping,
  thawed (about 1¾ cups)
  Flaked coconut

1. In medium saucepan, combine EAGLE BRAND®, egg yolks, lemon juice, lemon rind (optional) and food coloring (optional). Over medium heat, cook and stir until slightly thickened, about 10 minutes. Chill.

2. Preheat oven to 350°F. Prepare cake mix as package directs. Pour batter into greased and floured two 9-inch round layer cake pans.

3. Bake 30 minutes or until toothpick inserted near centers comes out clean. Remove from pans. Cool.

4. With sharp knife, remove crust from top of each cake. Split into layers. Spread equal portions of lemon mixture between layers and on top to within 1 inch of edge.

5. Frost side and 1-inch rim on top of cake with whipped topping. Coat side of cake with coconut; garnish as desired. Store leftovers covered in refrigerator.   *Makes one (9-inch) cake*

Prep Time: 15 minutes
Bake Time: 30 minutes

easy eggnog pound cake

1 (18.25- or 18.5-ounce) package yellow cake mix
1 (4-serving size) package instant vanilla pudding and
    pie filling mix
¾ cup BORDEN® EggNog
¾ cup vegetable oil
4 eggs
½ teaspoon ground nutmeg
    Powdered sugar (optional)

1. Preheat oven to 350°F.

2. In large bowl, combine cake mix, pudding mix, BORDEN® EggNog and oil; beat on low speed until moistened. Add eggs and nutmeg; beat at medium-high speed 4 minutes. Pour into greased and floured 10-inch fluted or tube pan.

3. Bake 40 to 45 minutes or until toothpick inserted near center comes out clean. Cool 10 minutes; remove from pan. Cool completely. Sprinkle with powdered sugar (optional). Store leftovers covered at room temperature.   *Makes one (10-inch) cake*

Prep Time: 10 minutes
Bake Time: 40 to 45 minutes

strawberry cream cheese shortcake

2 cups biscuit baking mix
2 tablespoons sugar
$\frac{1}{2}$ cup (1 stick) butter or margarine, softened
$\frac{1}{3}$ cup warm water
1 (8-ounce) package cream cheese, softened
1 (14-ounce) can EAGLE BRAND® Sweetened Condensed Milk
    (NOT evaporated milk)
$\frac{1}{3}$ cup lemon juice
1 teaspoon vanilla extract
1 quart (about 1$\frac{1}{2}$ pounds) fresh strawberries, cleaned, hulled
    and sliced
1 (13.5- or 16-ounce) package prepared strawberry glaze, chilled
    Whipped topping or whipped cream

1. Preheat oven to 400°F.

2. In small bowl, combine biscuit mix and sugar. Add butter and water; beat until well blended. Press on bottom of lightly greased 9-inch square baking pan.

3. Bake 10 to 12 minutes or until toothpick inserted near center comes out clean. Cool.

4. In large bowl, beat cream cheese until fluffy. Gradually beat in EAGLE BRAND® until smooth. Stir in lemon juice and vanilla. Spread evenly over shortcake layer. Chill at least 3 hours or until set. Cut into squares.

5. In bowl, combine strawberries and glaze. Spoon over shortcake just before serving. Garnish with whipped topping. Store leftovers covered in refrigerator. *Makes one (9-inch) cake*

Prep Time: 20 minutes
Bake Time: 10 to 12 minutes
Chill Time: 3 hours

peach cream cake

1 (10¾-ounce) loaf angel food cake, frozen
1 (14-ounce) can EAGLE BRAND® Sweetened Condensed Milk
    (NOT evaporated milk)
1 cup cold water
1 teaspoon almond extract
1 (4-serving size) package instant vanilla pudding and
    pie filling mix
2 cups (1 pint) whipping cream, whipped
4 cups sliced peeled fresh peaches (about 2 pounds)

1. Cut cake into ¼-inch slices; arrange half the slices on bottom of ungreased 13×9-inch baking dish.

2. In large bowl, combine EAGLE BRAND®, water and almond extract. Add pudding mix; beat well. Chill 5 minutes.

3. Fold in whipped cream. Spread half the cream mixture over cake slices; arrange half the peach slices on top. Top with remaining cake slices, cream filling and peach slices.

4. Chill 4 hours or until set. Cut into squares to serve. Store leftovers covered in refrigerator.   *Makes one (13×9-inch) cake*

Prep Time: 25 minutes
Chill Time: 4 hours 5 minutes

rich caramel cake

1 (14-ounce) package caramels, unwrapped
$^{1}/_{2}$ cup (1 stick) butter or margarine
1 (14-ounce) can EAGLE BRAND® Sweetened Condensed Milk
    (NOT evaporated milk)
1 (18.25- or 18.5-ounce) package chocolate cake mix, plus
    ingredients to prepare mix
1 cup coarsely chopped pecans

1. Preheat oven to 350°F. In heavy saucepan over low heat, melt caramels and butter. Remove from heat; add EAGLE BRAND®. Mix well; set aside.

2. Prepare cake mix as package directs. Spread 2 cups cake batter into greased 13×9-inch baking pan; bake 15 minutes.

3. Spread caramel mixture evenly over cake; spread remaining cake batter over caramel mixture. Top with pecans.

4. Bake 30 to 35 minutes or until toothpick inserted into center comes out clean. Cool. Store leftovers covered in refrigerator.

Makes one (13×9-inch) cake

Prep Time: 25 minutes
Bake Time: 45 to 50 minutes

cool and minty party cake

1 (14-ounce) can EAGLE BRAND® Sweetened Condensed Milk
(NOT evaporated milk)
2 teaspoons peppermint extract
8 drops green food coloring (optional)
2 cups (1 pint) whipping cream, whipped (do not use non-dairy
whipped topping)
1 (18.25- or 18.5-ounce) package white cake mix, plus
ingredients to prepare mix
Green crème de menthe liqueur
1 (8-ounce) container frozen non-dairy whipped topping, thawed

1. In large bowl, combine EAGLE BRAND®, peppermint extract and
food coloring (optional). Fold in whipped cream. Pour into foil-lined
9-inch round cake pan; cover. Freeze at least 6 hours or until firm.

2. Prepare and bake cake mix as package directs for two 9-inch round
layers. Remove from pans; cool completely.

3. With fork, poke holes in cake layers, 1 inch apart, halfway through
each layer. Spoon small amounts of liqueur into holes. Place one cake
layer on serving plate; top with frozen EAGLE BRAND® mixture, then
second cake layer. Trim frozen layer to edge of cake layers.

4. Frost quickly with whipped topping. Return to freezer for at least
6 hours before serving. Garnish as desired. Store leftovers covered in
freezer. *Makes one (9-inch) cake*

Prep Time: 20 minutes
Freeze Time: 12 hours

chocolate almond torte

   4 eggs, separated
   1 cup sugar
   ¹/₂ cup (1 stick) butter or margarine, softened
   1 teaspoon *each* almond extract and vanilla extract
   1 cup finely chopped toasted almonds
   ³/₄ cup all-purpose flour
   ¹/₂ cup unsweetened cocoa
   ¹/₂ teaspoon *each* baking powder and baking soda
   ²/₃ cup milk
   Chocolate Almond Frosting (recipe follows)

1. Preheat oven to 350°F. In small bowl, beat egg whites until soft peaks form; set aside.

2. In large bowl, beat sugar and butter until fluffy. Add egg yolks and extracts; mix well. In medium bowl, combine almonds, flour, cocoa, baking powder and baking soda; add alternately with milk to butter mixture, beating well after each addition. Fold in beaten egg whites. Pour into 2 (8- or 9-inch) round wax paper-lined cake pans.

3. Bake 18 to 20 minutes or until toothpick inserted near centers comes out clean. Cool 10 minutes; remove from pans. Cool completely.

4. Prepare Chocolate Almond Frosting. Split each cake layer; fill and frost with frosting. Garnish as desired. Store leftovers covered in refrigerator. *Makes one (4-layer) cake*

Prep Time: 30 minutes
Bake Time: 18 to 20 minutes

chocolate almond frosting

   2 (1-ounce) squares semisweet chocolate, chopped
   1 (14-ounce) can EAGLE BRAND® Sweetened Condensed Milk
      (NOT evaporated milk)
   1 teaspoon almond extract

1. In heavy saucepan over medium heat, melt chocolate with EAGLE BRAND®. Cook and stir until mixture thickens, about 10 minutes.

2. Remove from heat; cool 10 minutes. Stir in almond extract; cool.
Makes about 1¹/₂ cups

fudge ribbon cake

1 (18.25- or 18.5 ounce) package chocolate cake mix
1 (8-ounce) package cream cheese, softened
2 tablespoons butter or margarine, softened
1 tablespoon cornstarch
1 (14-ounce) can EAGLE BRAND® Sweetened Condensed Milk
   (NOT evaporated milk)
1 egg
1 teaspoon vanilla extract
   Chocolate Glaze (recipe follows) or powdered sugar (optional)

1. Preheat oven to 350°F. Prepare cake mix as package directs. Pour batter into greased and floured 13×9-inch baking pan.

2. In small bowl, beat cream cheese, butter and cornstarch until fluffy. Gradually beat in EAGLE BRAND® until smooth. Add egg and vanilla; mix well. Spoon evenly over cake batter.

3. Bake 40 minutes or until toothpick inserted near center comes out clean. Cool. Drizzle with chocolate glaze or sprinkle with powdered sugar (optional). Store leftovers covered in refrigerator.

Makes one (13×9-inch) cake

Prep Time: 20 minutes
Bake Time: 40 minutes

chocolate glaze: In small saucepan over low heat, melt 1 (1-ounce) square unsweetened or semisweet chocolate and 1 tablespoon butter or margarine with 2 tablespoons water. Remove from heat. Stir in ³/₄ cup powdered sugar and ¹/₂ teaspoon vanilla extract. Stir until smooth and well blended. Makes about ¹/₃ cup glaze.

serving suggestion: Invert slices on serving plate as shown in photo; garnish as desired.

fudge ribbon bundt cake: Preheat oven to 350°F. Grease and flour 10-inch bundt pan. Prepare cake mix as package directs. Pour batter into prepared pan. Prepare cream cheese layer as directed above; spoon evenly over batter. Bake 50 to 55 minutes or until toothpick inserted near center comes out clean. Cool 10 minutes. Remove from pan. Cool. Prepare Chocolate Glaze and drizzle over cake. Store leftovers covered in refrigerator.

holiday coffeecake

    2 cups biscuit baking mix
    1 (14-ounce) can EAGLE BRAND® Sweetened Condensed Milk
       (NOT evaporated milk)
    ³/₄ cup sour cream
    ¼ cup (½ stick) plus 1 tablespoon butter or margarine, melted
       and divided
    2 eggs
 1½ teaspoons ground cinnamon, divided
    ½ cup chopped pecans
    2 tablespoons firmly packed light brown sugar

1. Preheat oven to 350°F.

2. In large bowl, beat biscuit mix, EAGLE BRAND®, sour cream, butter, eggs and ½ teaspoon cinnamon until smooth. Pour batter into lightly greased 11×7-inch baking dish.

3. In small bowl, combine pecans, brown sugar, remaining 1 tablespoon butter and remaining 1 teaspoon cinnamon. Sprinkle mixture evenly over batter.

4. Bake 40 to 45 minutes or until toothpick inserted near center comes out clean. Cool in dish on wire rack 10 minutes. Store leftovers covered at room temperature. *Makes one (11×7-inch) cake*

Prep Time: 15 minutes
Bake Time: 40 to 45 minutes

german chocolate cake

1 (18.25- or 18.5-ounce) package German chocolate cake mix
1 cup water
3 eggs, plus 1 egg yolk
1/2 cup vegetable oil
1 (14-ounce) can EAGLE BRAND® Sweetened Condensed Milk
   (NOT evaporated milk), divided
3 tablespoons butter or margarine
1 egg yolk
1/3 cup chopped pecans
1/3 cup flaked coconut
1 teaspoon vanilla extract

1. Preheat oven to 350°F.

2. In large bowl, combine cake mix, water, 3 eggs, oil and 1/3 cup EAGLE BRAND®. Beat on low speed until moistened, then beat on high speed 2 minutes. Pour into well-greased and floured 13×9-inch baking pan.

3. Bake 40 to 45 minutes or until toothpick inserted near center comes out clean.

4. In small saucepan over low heat, combine remaining EAGLE BRAND®, butter and egg yolk. Cook and stir until thickened, about 6 minutes. Add pecans, coconut and vanilla; spread over warm cake. Store leftovers covered in refrigerator.

Makes one (13×9-inch) cake

Prep Time: 15 minutes
Bake Time: 40 to 45 minutes

holiday mini cherry pound cakes

2³/₄ cups sugar
1¹/₄ cups (2¹/₂ sticks) butter or margarine, softened
5 eggs
1 teaspoon vanilla extract
3 cups all-purpose flour
1 teaspoon baking powder
¹/₄ teaspoon salt
1 (14-ounce) can EAGLE BRAND® Sweetened Condensed Milk
  (NOT evaporated milk)
2 cups quartered maraschino cherries, well drained

1. Preheat oven to 350°F.

2. In large bowl with electric mixer on low speed, beat sugar, butter, eggs and vanilla until blended, then on high speed 5 minutes until light and fluffy.

3. Combine flour, baking powder and salt. Add flour mixture alternately with EAGLE BRAND® to creamed mixture, mixing lightly after each addition. Fold in cherries. Turn batter into 6 greased and floured mini (5×3-inch) loaf pans.

4. Bake 45 minutes or until light brown. Let cool in pan 5 minutes; invert loaves onto rack and let cool completely. Store leftovers covered at room temperature.   *Makes 6 mini loaves*

Prep Time: 25 minutes
Bake Time: 45 minutes

 Create delicious homemade gifts by baking cakes in decorative aluminum loaf pans and wrapping with a festive bow.

chocolate sheet cake

1¼ cups (2½ sticks) butter or margarine, divided
  1 cup water
  ½ cup unsweetened cocoa, divided
  2 cups all-purpose flour
1¼ cups firmly packed light brown sugar
  1 teaspoon baking soda
  1 teaspoon ground cinnamon
  ½ teaspoon salt
  1 (14-ounce) can EAGLE BRAND® Sweetened Condensed Milk
    (NOT evaporated milk), divided
  2 eggs
  1 teaspoon vanilla extract
  1 cup powdered sugar
  1 cup coarsely chopped nuts

1. Preheat oven to 350°F. In small saucepan over medium heat, melt 1 cup (2 sticks) butter; stir in water and ¼ cup cocoa. Bring to a boil; remove from heat.

2. In large bowl, combine flour, brown sugar, baking soda, cinnamon and salt. Add cocoa mixture; beat well. Stir in ⅓ cup EAGLE BRAND®, eggs and vanilla. Pour into ungreased 15×10×1-inch baking pan.

3. Bake 15 minutes or until cake springs back when lightly touched.

4. In small saucepan over medium heat, melt remaining ¼ cup (½ stick) butter; add remaining ¼ cup cocoa and remaining EAGLE BRAND®. Stir in powdered sugar and nuts. Spread over warm cake. Store leftovers covered at room temperature.   *Makes one (15×10-inch) cake*

Prep Time: 25 minutes
Bake Time: 15 minutes

fruit pie frenzy

banana coconut cream pie

　　3 tablespoons cornstarch
　1⅓ cups water
　　1 (14-ounce) can EAGLE BRAND® Sweetened Condensed Milk
　　　　(NOT evaporated milk)
　　3 egg yolks, beaten
　　2 tablespoons butter or margarine
　　1 teaspoon vanilla extract
　½ cup flaked coconut, toasted
　　2 medium bananas
　　2 tablespoons lemon juice
　　1 (9-inch) prepared graham cracker or baked pie crust
　　　Whipped cream (optional)
　　　Additional toasted coconut for garnish (optional)

1. In heavy saucepan over medium heat, dissolve cornstarch in water; stir in EAGLE BRAND® and egg yolks. Cook and stir until thickened and bubbly. Remove from heat; add butter and vanilla. Cool slightly. Fold in coconut; set aside.

2. Peel and slice bananas into ¼-inch-thick rounds. Toss banana slices gently with lemon juice; drain. Arrange bananas on bottom of crust. Pour filling over bananas.

3. Cover; refrigerate 4 hours or until set. Top with whipped cream and additional toasted coconut (optional). Store leftovers covered in refrigerator.　　　　　　　　　　　　　　*Makes one (9-inch) pie*

Prep Time: 15 minutes
Chill Time: 4 hours

cherry-topped lemon cheesecake pie

1 (8-ounce) package cream cheese, softened
1 (14-ounce) can EAGLE BRAND® Sweetened Condensed Milk
    (NOT evaporated milk)
⅓ cup lemon juice
1 teaspoon vanilla extract
1 (6-ounce) prepared graham cracker pie crust
1 (21-ounce) can cherry pie filling, chilled

1. In large bowl, beat cream cheese until fluffy. Gradually beat in EAGLE BRAND® until smooth. Add lemon juice and vanilla; mix well. Pour into crust.

2. Chill at least 3 hours. To serve, top with cherry pie filling. Store leftovers covered in refrigerator.   *Makes one (6-ounce) pie*

Prep Time: 10 minutes
Chill Time: 3 hours

note: For a firmer crust, brush crust with beaten egg white; bake in preheated 375°F oven 5 minutes. Cool before pouring filling into crust.

apple cranberry streusel custard pie

1 (14-ounce) can EAGLE BRAND® Sweetened Condensed Milk
    (NOT evaporated milk)
1 teaspoon ground cinnamon
2 eggs, beaten
1/2 cup hot water
1 1/2 cups fresh or frozen cranberries
2 medium all-purpose apples, peeled and sliced (about 1 1/2 cups)
1 (9-inch) unbaked pie crust
1/2 cup firmly packed light brown sugar
1/2 cup all-purpose flour
1/4 cup (1/2 stick) butter or margarine, softened
1/2 cup chopped nuts

1. Place rack in lower third of oven; preheat oven to 425°F.

2. In large bowl, combine EAGLE BRAND® and cinnamon. Add eggs, water and fruits; mix well. Pour into crust.

3. In medium bowl, combine brown sugar and flour; cut in butter until crumbly. Add nuts. Sprinkle over pie. Bake 10 minutes.

4. Reduce oven temperature to 375°F; continue baking 30 to 40 minutes or until golden brown. Cool. Store covered in refrigerator.

Makes one (9-inch) pie

Prep Time: 25 minutes
Bake Time: 40 to 50 minutes

lemon icebox pie

1 (14-ounce) can EAGLE BRAND® Sweetened Condensed Milk (NOT evaporated milk)
½ cup lemon juice
Yellow food coloring (optional)
1 cup (½ pint) whipping cream, whipped
1 (6-ounce) prepared graham cracker or baked pie crust

1. In medium bowl, combine EAGLE BRAND®, lemon juice and food coloring (optional). Fold in whipped cream. Pour into crust.

2. Chill 3 hours or until set. Garnish as desired. Store leftovers covered in refrigerator.   *Makes one (6-ounce) pie*

Prep Time: 10 minutes
Chill Time: 3 hours

One fresh lemon equals 3 tablespoons of juice. To equal ½ cup lemon juice for this recipe, three lemons will be needed.

perfect pumpkin pie

    1 (15-ounce) can pumpkin (about 2 cups)
    1 (14-ounce) can EAGLE BRAND® Sweetened Condensed Milk
       (NOT evaporated milk)
    2 eggs
    1 teaspoon ground cinnamon
    $1/2$ teaspoon ground ginger
    $1/2$ teaspoon ground nutmeg
    $1/2$ teaspoon salt
    1 (9-inch) unbaked pie crust

1. Preheat oven to 425°F.

2. In medium bowl, whisk pumpkin, EAGLE BRAND®, eggs, cinnamon, ginger, nutmeg and salt until smooth. Pour into crust. Bake 15 minutes.

3. Reduce oven temperature to 350°F and continue baking 35 to 40 minutes longer or until knife inserted 1 inch from crust comes out clean. Cool. Garnish as desired. Store leftovers covered in refrigerator.

Makes one (9-inch) pie

Prep Time: 15 minutes
Bake Time: 50 to 55 minutes

sour cream topping: In medium bowl, combine $1 1/2$ cups sour cream, 2 tablespoons sugar and 1 teaspoon vanilla extract. After pie has baked 30 minutes at 350°F, spread mixture evenly over top; bake 10 minutes longer. Makes about $1 3/4$ cups.

streusel topping: In medium bowl, combine $1/2$ cup packed brown sugar and $1/2$ cup all-purpose flour; cut in $1/4$ cup ($1/2$ stick) cold butter or margarine until crumbly. Stir in $1/4$ cup chopped nuts. After pie has baked 30 minutes at 350°F, sprinkle streusel evenly over top; bake 10 minutes longer. Makes about 2 cups.

apple custard tart

  1 folded refrigerated unbaked pie crust (one-half of 15-ounce
    package)
  1 (14-ounce) can EAGLE BRAND® Sweetened Condensed Milk
    (NOT evaporated milk)
1½ cups sour cream
  ¼ cup frozen apple juice concentrate, thawed
  1 egg
1½ teaspoons vanilla extract
  ¼ teaspoon ground cinnamon
  2 medium all-purpose apples, cored, peeled and thinly sliced
  1 tablespoon butter or margarine
    Apple Cinnamon Glaze (recipe follows)

1. Let refrigerated pie crust stand at room temperature according to package directions. Preheat oven to 375°F. On floured surface, roll pie crust from center to edge, forming circle about 13 inches in diameter. Ease pastry into 11-inch tart pan with removable bottom. Trim pastry even with rim of pan. Place pan on baking sheet. Bake crust 15 minutes or until lightly browned.

2. In small bowl, beat EAGLE BRAND®, sour cream, apple juice concentrate, egg, vanilla and cinnamon until smooth. Pour into crust.

3. Bake 25 minutes or until center appears set when shaken. Cool 1 hour on wire rack.

4. In large skillet, cook apples in butter until tender-crisp. Arrange apples on top of tart; drizzle with Apple Cinnamon Glaze. Chill in refrigerator at least 4 hours. Store leftovers covered in refrigerator.

Makes one (11-inch) tart

Prep Time: 10 minutes
Bake Time: 40 minutes
Cool Time: 1 hour
Chill Time: 4 hours

apple cinnamon glaze: In small saucepan over low heat, combine ⅓ cup apple juice concentrate, 1 teaspoon ground cinnamon, mix well. Cook and stir until thick and bubbly. Makes about ⅓ cup.

creamy lemon pie

3 egg yolks
1 (14-ounce) can EAGLE BRAND® Sweetened Condensed Milk
    (NOT evaporated milk)
½ cup lemon juice
1 (8- or 9-inch) prepared graham cracker or baked pie crust
    Whipped topping or whipped cream
    Lemon curl or grated lemon rind (optional)

1. Preheat oven to 325°F.

2. In medium bowl; beat egg yolks; gradually beat in EAGLE BRAND® and lemon juice. Pour into crust.

3. Bake 30 to 35 minutes or until set. Remove from oven. Cool 1 hour. Chill at least 3 hours.

4. Before serving, spread whipped topping over pie. Garnish with lemon curl or rind (optional). Store leftovers covered in refrigerator.

Makes one (8- or 9-inch) pie

Prep Time: 15 minutes
Bake Time: 30 to 35 minutes
Cool Time: 1 hour
Chill Time: 3 hours

 To make a lemon curl, cut a strip of lemon rind—yellow part only—using a paring knife or zester. Wind around a straw or chopstick, and secure with plastic wrap. Let stand 1 hour. To use, unwrap, slide the curl off the straw, and arrange attractively.

banana pudding cream pie

1½ cups vanilla wafer crumbs (about 36 wafers)
⅓ cup butter or margarine, melted
¼ cup sugar
1 (14-ounce) can EAGLE BRAND® Sweetened Condensed Milk
(NOT evaporated milk)
4 egg yolks
1 (4-serving size) package cook-and-serve vanilla pudding mix
½ cup water
1 (8-ounce) container sour cream, at room temperature
2 medium bananas, sliced, dipped in lemon juice and drained
Whipped cream
Additional banana slices, dipped in lemon juice and drained
Additional vanilla wafers

1. Preheat oven to 375°F. Combine wafer crumbs, butter and sugar; press firmly on bottom and up side to rim of ungreased 9-inch pie plate to form crust. Bake 8 to 10 minutes. Cool.

2. In heavy saucepan, combine EAGLE BRAND®, egg yolks, pudding mix and water; stir until well blended. Over medium heat, cook and stir until thickened and bubbly. Cool 15 minutes. Beat in sour cream.

3. Arrange banana slices on bottom of baked crust. Pour filling over bananas; cover. Chill. Top with whipped cream. Garnish with additional banana slices and vanilla wafers. Store leftovers covered in refrigerator.

Makes one (9-inch) pie

Prep Time: 20 minutes
Bake Time: 8 to 10 minutes

cranberry crumb pie

1 (9-inch) unbaked pie crust
1 (8-ounce) package cream cheese, softened
1 (14-ounce) can EAGLE BRAND® Sweetened Condensed Milk
    (NOT evaporated milk)
¼ cup lemon juice
3 tablespoons light brown sugar, divided
2 tablespoons cornstarch
1 (16-ounce) can whole berry cranberry sauce
¼ cup (½ stick) cold butter or margarine
⅓ cup all-purpose flour
¾ cup chopped walnuts

1. Preheat oven to 425°F. Bake pie crust 6 minutes; remove from oven. Reduce oven temperature to 375°F.

2. In large bowl, beat cream cheese until fluffy. Gradually beat in EAGLE BRAND® until smooth. Add lemon juice; mix well. Pour into baked crust.

3. In small bowl, combine 1 tablespoon brown sugar and cornstarch; mix well. Stir in cranberry sauce. Spoon evenly over cheese mixture.

4. In medium bowl, cut butter into flour and remaining 2 tablespoons brown sugar until crumbly. Stir in walnuts. Sprinkle evenly over cranberry mixture. Bake 45 to 50 minutes or until bubbly and golden. Cool. Serve at room temperature or chill. Store leftovers covered in refrigerator.   *Makes one (9-inch) pie*

Prep Time: 20 minutes
Bake Time: 51 to 56 minutes

key lime pie

   3 eggs, separated
   1 (14-ounce) can EAGLE BRAND® Sweetened Condensed Milk
      (NOT evaporated milk)
   1/2 cup key lime juice
   2 to 3 drops green food coloring (optional)
   1 (9-inch) unbaked pie crust
   1/4 teaspoon cream of tartar
   1/3 cup sugar

1. Preheat oven to 325°F.

2. In medium bowl, beat egg yolks; gradually beat in EAGLE BRAND® and lime juice. Stir in food coloring (optional). Pour into pie crust. Bake 30 minutes. Remove from oven. Increase oven temperature to 350°F.

3. In large bowl beat egg whites and cream of tartar on high until soft peaks form. Gradually beat in sugar on medium speed, 1 tablespoon at a time; beat 4 minutes or until sugar is dissolved and stiff glossy peaks form.

4. Immediately spread meringue over hot pie, carefully sealing to edge of crust to prevent meringue from shrinking. Bake 15 minutes. Cool 1 hour. Chill at least 3 hours. Store leftovers covered in refrigerator.

Makes one (9-inch) pie

Prep Time: 10 minutes
Bake Time: 45 minutes
Cool Time: 1 hour
Chill Time: 3 hours

magic lemon pie

1 (14-ounce) can EAGLE BRAND® Sweetened Condensed Milk
    (NOT evaporated milk)
1/2 cup lemon juice
1 teaspoon grated lemon rind *or* 1/4 teaspoon lemon extract
2 eggs, separated
1 (8- or 9-inch) prepared graham cracker or baked pie crust
1/4 teaspoon cream of tartar
1/4 cup sugar

1. Preheat oven to 325°F.

2. In medium bowl, combine EAGLE BRAND®, lemon juice, lemon rind or extract and egg yolks; stir until mixture thickens. Pour into chilled graham cracker crust or cooled pie crust.

3. In medium bowl, beat egg whites and cream of tartar on high speed until soft peaks form. Gradually beat in sugar on medium speed, 1 tablespoon at a time; beat 4 minutes longer or until sugar is dissolved and stiff glossy peaks form.

4. Spread meringue over pie, carefully sealing over edge of crust to prevent meringue from shrinking. Bake 12 to 15 minutes or until meringue is lightly browned. Cool. Store leftovers covered in refrigerator.

Makes one (9-inch) pie

Prep Time: 10 minutes
Bake Time: 12 to 15 minutes

Table of Contents

frozen delights

classic vanilla ice cream

1 vanilla bean _or_ 2 tablespoons vanilla extract
2 cups (1 pint) half-and-half
2 cups (1 pint) whipping cream
1 (14-ounce) can EAGLE BRAND® Sweetened Condensed Milk
(NOT evaporated milk)

1. Split vanilla bean lengthwise and scrape out seeds or use vanilla extract. In large bowl, combine vanilla seeds or extract, half-and-half, whipping cream and EAGLE BRAND®; mix well.

2. Pour into ice cream freezer container. Freeze according to manufacturer's instructions. Store leftovers covered in freezer.

Makes about 1 1/2 quarts

refrigerator-freezer method: Omit half-and-half. Whip whipping cream. In large bowl, combine EAGLE BRAND® and vanilla. Fold in whipped cream. Pour into 9×5-inch loaf pan or other 2-quart container. Cover. Freeze 6 hours or until firm. Store leftovers covered in freezer.

fantastic sundaes: Top scoops of vanilla ice cream with flavored syrups, fresh fruits, crushed candies or crumbled cookies. Add a dollop of whipped cream and the ever-popular cherry.

homemade ice cream sandwiches: Place a scoop of vanilla ice cream on a homemade or packaged cookie; top with another cookie. For a festive touch, roll the sandwich edge in crushed candy, chopped nuts or toasted coconut. Wrap individually in foil and freeze.

à la mode desserts: Design your own signature desserts by topping brownies, waffles or pound cake slices with a scoop of vanilla ice cream and fresh fruit, syrup or nuts.

delicious homemade milk shakes: Combine 2 large scoops of vanilla ice cream with 1 cup milk in blender; blend in flavored syrups or fruits if desired.

Prep Time: 10 minutes

frozen mocha cheesecake loaf

2 cups finely crushed crème-filled chocolate sandwich cookies
(about 24 cookies)
3 tablespoons butter or margarine, melted
1 (8-ounce) package cream cheese, softened
1 (14-ounce) can EAGLE BRAND® Sweetened Condensed Milk
(NOT evaporated milk)
1 tablespoon vanilla extract
2 cups (1 pint) whipping cream, whipped
2 tablespoons instant coffee
1 tablespoon hot water
$\frac{1}{2}$ cup chocolate syrup

1. Line 9×5-inch loaf pan with foil, extending foil over sides of pan. In small bowl, combine cookie crumbs and butter; press firmly on bottom and halfway up sides of prepared pan.

2. In large bowl, beat cream cheese until fluffy. Gradually beat in EAGLE BRAND® until smooth. Stir in vanilla; mix well. Fold in whipped cream.

3. Remove half the mixture and place in medium bowl. In small bowl, dissolve coffee in water. Fold in coffee mixture and chocolate syrup. Spoon half the chocolate mixture into crust, then half the vanilla mixture. Repeat. With knife, swirl through cream mixture to marble.

4. Cover; freeze 6 hours or until firm. To serve, remove from pan; peel off foil. Cut into slices and garnish as desired. Store leftovers covered in freezer.   *Makes one (9×5-inch) loaf*

Prep Time: 20 minutes
Freeze Time: 6 hours

chocolate ice cream cups

　　2 cups (12 ounces) semisweet chocolate chips
　　1 (14-ounce) can EAGLE BRAND® Sweetened Condensed Milk
　　　　(NOT evaporated milk)
　　1 cup finely ground pecans
　　　Ice cream, any flavor

1. In large heavy saucepan over low heat, melt chocolate chips with EAGLE BRAND®; remove from heat. Stir in pecans. In individual paper-lined muffin cups, pour about 2 tablespoons chocolate mixture. With lightly greased spoon, spread chocolate on bottom and up side of each cup.

2. Freeze 2 hours or until firm. Before serving, remove paper liners. Fill chocolate cups with ice cream. Store unfilled cups tightly covered in freezer.　　　　　　　　　　　　　*Makes about 1 1/2 dozen cups*

Prep Time: 20 minutes
Freeze Time: 2 hours

 It is easier to remove the paper liners if the chocolate cups sit at room temperature for about 5 minutes first.

strawberry sundae dessert

1 (9-ounce) package chocolate wafers, finely crushed
   (2 cups crumbs)
½ cup (1 stick) butter or margarine, melted
1 (14-ounce) can EAGLE BRAND® Sweetened Condensed Milk
   (NOT evaporated milk)
1 tablespoon vanilla extract
2 cups (1 pint) whipping cream, whipped
2 (10-ounce) packages frozen strawberries, thawed (5 cups)
¼ cup sugar
1 tablespoon lemon juice
2 teaspoons cornstarch

1. In small bowl, combine wafer crumbs and butter. Press half the crumb mixture on bottom of 9-inch square baking pan.

2. In large bowl, combine EAGLE BRAND® and vanilla. Fold in whipped cream. Pour into crust.

3. In blender or food processor, combine strawberries, sugar and lemon juice; blend until smooth. Spoon ¾ cup strawberry mixture evenly over cream mixture. Top with remaining crumb mixture. Cover; freeze 6 hours or until firm.

4. In small saucepan over medium heat, combine remaining strawberry mixture and cornstarch. Cook and stir until thickened. Cool. Chill.

5. Cut dessert into squares; serve with sauce. Store leftovers covered in freezer; refrigerate any leftover sauce. *Makes 6 to 9 squares*

Prep Time: 20 minutes
Freeze Time: 6 hours

crunchy peppermint candy ice cream

2 cups (1 pint) light cream
1 (14-ounce) can EAGLE BRAND® Sweetened Condensed Milk
   (NOT evaporated milk)
1¼ cups water
½ cup crushed hard peppermint candy
1 tablespoon vanilla extract

1. Combine cream, EAGLE BRAND®, water, candy and vanilla in ice cream freezer container. Freeze according to manufacturer's instructions.

2. Garnish with additional crushed peppermint candy (optional). Store leftovers tightly covered in freezer. *Makes 1½ quarts*

Prep Time: 15 minutes

 To easily crush the hard peppermint candy, place it in a resealable food storage bag and seal bag. Place bag between 2 sheets of waxed paper and crush with a rolling pin or meat mallet.

ambrosia freeze

1 (8-ounce) container strawberry cream cheese
2 medium bananas, mashed
1 (14-ounce) can EAGLE BRAND® Sweetened Condensed Milk
    (NOT evaporated milk)
1 (8-ounce) container strawberry yogurt
2 tablespoons lemon juice
1 (11-ounce) can mandarin orange sections, drained
1 (8-ounce) can crushed pineapple, well drained
½ cup toasted flaked coconut
    Red food coloring (optional)

1. In large bowl with electric mixer on low speed, beat cream cheese and bananas until smooth. Beat in EAGLE BRAND®, yogurt and lemon juice until blended. Stir in orange sections, pineapple and coconut. Stir in food coloring (optional). Spoon into ungreased 11×7-inch baking dish.

2. Cover and freeze 6 hours or until firm. Remove from freezer 15 minutes before serving. Cut into 1×1-inch cubes; serve in dessert dishes or stemmed glasses. *Makes 8 to 10 servings*

Prep Time: 20 minutes
Freeze Time: 6 hours

peppermint ice cream gems

3 cups finely crushed crème-filled chocolate sandwich cookies
   (about 36 cookies)
$^1/_2$ cup (1 stick) butter or margarine, melted
1 (14-ounce) can EAGLE BRAND® Sweetened Condensed Milk
   (NOT evaporated milk)
$^1/_4$ cup white crème de menthe liqueur or $^1/_2$ teaspoon
   peppermint extract
2 tablespoons peppermint Schnapps
1 to 2 drops red or green food coloring (optional)
2 cups (1 pint) whipping cream, whipped (NOT nondairy
   whipped topping)

1. In medium bowl, combine cookie crumbs and butter. Press
2 rounded tablespoons crumb mixture in bottom and up sides of
24 standard ($2^1/_2$-inch) paper-lined muffin cups.

2. In large bowl, combine EAGLE BRAND®, crème de menthe,
Schnapps and food coloring (optional). Fold in whipped cream.
Spoon mixture into crusts.

3. Freeze 6 hours or until firm. To serve, remove paper liners. Garnish
as desired. Store leftovers covered in freezer.   *Makes 2 dozen gems*

Prep Time: 25 minutes
Freeze Time: 6 hours

double chocolate ice cream squares

1½ cups finely crushed crème-filled chocolate sandwich cookies
    (about 18 cookies)
2 to 3 tablespoons butter or margarine, melted
1 (14-ounce) can EAGLE BRAND® Sweetened Condensed Milk
    (NOT evaporated milk)
3 (1-ounce) squares unsweetened chocolate, melted
2 teaspoons vanilla extract
1 cup chopped nuts (optional)
2 cups (1 pint) whipping cream, whipped
2 cups whipped topping
    Additional chopped nuts (optional)

1. In medium bowl, combine cookie crumbs and butter; press firmly on bottom of ungreased 13×9-inch baking pan.

2. In large bowl, beat EAGLE BRAND®, melted chocolate and vanilla until well blended. Stir in nuts (optional). Fold in whipped cream. Pour into crust. Spread with whipped topping.

3. Cover; freeze 6 hours or until firm. Garnish with additional chopped nuts (optional) or as desired. Store leftovers covered in freezer. *Makes about 1 dozen squares*

Prep Time: 20 minutes
Freeze Time: 6 hours

rocky road ice cream squares: Add 1 cup miniature marshmallows to EAGLE BRAND® mixture. Proceed as directed above.

frozen peppermint cheesecake

2 cups finely crushed chocolate wafer cookies or crème-filled
    chocolate sandwich cookies (about 24 cookies)
$\frac{1}{4}$ cup sugar
$\frac{1}{4}$ cup ($\frac{1}{2}$ stick) butter or margarine, melted
1 (8-ounce) package cream cheese, softened
1 (14-ounce) can EAGLE BRAND® Sweetened Condensed Milk
    (NOT evaporated milk)
2 teaspoons peppermint extract
    Red food coloring (optional)
2 cups whipping cream, whipped
    Hot fudge ice cream topping (optional)

1. In medium bowl, combine cookie crumbs and sugar. Add butter; mix well. Press 2 cups crumb mixture firmly on bottom and halfway up side of foil-lined 9-inch round cake or springform pan. Chill.

2. In large bowl, beat cream cheese until fluffy. Gradually beat in EAGLE BRAND® until smooth. Stir in peppermint extract and food coloring (optional); mix well. Fold in whipped cream. Pour into crust.

3. Cover; freeze 6 hours or until firm. Garnish with topping (optional). Store leftovers covered in freezer.

Makes one (9-inch) cheesecake

Prep Time: 20 minutes
Freeze Time: 6 hours

candy & fudge

creamy almond candy

1½ pounds vanilla-flavored candy coating*
1 (14-ounce) can EAGLE BRAND® Sweetened Condensed Milk
     (NOT evaporated milk)
⅛ teaspoon salt
3 cups (about 1 pound) whole almonds, toasted**
1 teaspoon almond extract

*Also called confectioners' coating or almond bark. If it is not available in your local supermarket, it can be purchased in candy specialty stores.

**To toast almonds, spread in single layer in heavy-bottomed skillet. Cook over medium heat 2 to 3 minutes, stirring frequently, until nuts are lightly browned. Remove from skillet immediately. Cool before using.

1. In large heavy saucepan over low heat, melt candy coating with EAGLE BRAND® and salt. Remove from heat; stir in almonds and almond extract. Spread evenly into wax paper-lined 15×10-inch jellyroll pan.

2. Chill 2 hours or until firm. Turn candy onto cutting board; peel off paper and cut into triangles or squares. Store leftovers tightly covered at room temperature.   *Makes about 3¼ pounds candy*

Prep Time: 10 minutes
Chill Time: 2 hours

microwave method: In 2-quart glass measure, combine candy coating, EAGLE BRAND® and salt. Microwave on HIGH (100% power) 3 to 5 minutes, stirring after each 1½ minutes. Stir until smooth. Proceed as directed above.

strawberry bon bons

1 (14-ounce) can EAGLE BRAND® Sweetened Condensed Milk
   (NOT evaporated milk)
1 (14-ounce) package flaked coconut
1 cup ground blanched almonds
1 (6-ounce) package strawberry-flavored gelatin, divided
1 teaspoon almond extract
   Red food coloring
2 cups powdered sugar
$\frac{1}{2}$ cup whipping cream
   Green food coloring

1. In large bowl, combine EAGLE BRAND®, coconut, almonds, $\frac{1}{3}$ cup gelatin, almond extract and enough red food coloring to tint mixture to desired red shade. Transfer mixture to food processor and pulse several times to form paste. Chill until firm enough to handle.

2. Shape spoonfuls of coconut mixture (about $\frac{3}{4}$ tablespoon) into strawberry shapes. Sprinkle remaining gelatin on flat dish; roll each strawberry in gelatin to coat. Place on wax paper-lined baking sheet; chill.

3. To make frosting "hulls," combine powdered sugar, whipping cream and green food coloring until well blended. Fill pastry bag fitted with open star tip with frosting; pipe small amount on top of each strawberry to form hull. Store leftovers tightly covered in refrigerator.

Makes about $2\frac{1}{2}$ pounds or 4 dozen bon bons

candy crunch

(pictured at right)

> 4 cups (half of 15-ounce bag) pretzel sticks or pretzel twists
> 4 cups (24 ounces) white chocolate chips
> 1 (14-ounce) can EAGLE BRAND® Sweetened Condensed Milk
>   (NOT evaporated milk)
> 1 cup dried fruit (dried cranberries, raisins or mixed dried fruit)

1. Place pretzels in large bowl.

2. In large saucepan over low heat, melt white chocolate chips with EAGLE BRAND®. Cook and stir constantly until smooth. Pour over pretzels, stirring to coat.

3. Immediately spread mixture into foil-lined 15×10-inch jellyroll pan. Sprinkle with dried fruit; press down lightly with back of spoon. Chill 1 to 2 hours or until set. Break into chunks. Store leftovers loosely covered at room temperature.   *Makes about 1³⁄₄ pounds candy*

Prep Time: 10 minutes
Chill Time: 1 to 2 hours

party mints

(pictured on page 248)

> 1 (14-ounce) can EAGLE BRAND® Sweetened Condensed Milk
>   (NOT evaporated milk)
> 1 (32-ounce) package powdered sugar
> ¹⁄₂ teaspoon peppermint extract
>   Assorted colored granulated sugar or crystals

1. In medium bowl, beat EAGLE BRAND® and half of powdered sugar until blended. Gradually add remaining powdered sugar and peppermint extract, beating until stiff.

2. Shape mixture into ¹⁄₂-inch balls. Roll in colored sugar; place on parchment paper. Let stand 8 hours to set. Store covered at room temperature.   *Makes 3 dozen mints*

Prep Time: 30 minutes
Stand Time: 8 hours

variation: You may also dip uncoated mints in melted chocolate.

chocolate snow swirl fudge

(pictured at right)

> 3 cups semisweet chocolate chips
> 1 (14-ounce) can EAGLE BRAND® Sweetened Condensed Milk
>   (NOT evaporated milk)
> 1/4 cup (1/2 stick) butter or margarine, divided
>   Dash salt
> 1 cup chopped nuts
> 1 1/2 teaspoons vanilla extract
> 2 cups miniature marshmallows

1. In large heavy saucepan over low heat, melt chocolate chips with EAGLE BRAND®, 2 tablespoons butter and salt. Remove from heat; stir in nuts and vanilla. Spread evenly in wax paper-lined 8- or 9-inch square pan.

2. In small saucepan over low heat, melt marshmallows with remaining 2 tablespoons butter; stir until smooth. Spread on top of fudge. With knife or metal spatula, swirl through swirl fudge to marble.

3. Chill at least 2 hours or until firm. Turn fudge onto cutting board; peel off paper and cut into squares. Store leftovers covered in refrigerator.

Makes about 2 pounds fudge

peanut butter fudge

> 1 (14-ounce) can EAGLE BRAND® Sweetened Condensed Milk
>   (NOT evaporated milk)
> 1/2 cup creamy peanut butter
> 2 (6-ounce) packages white chocolate squares, chopped
> 3/4 cup chopped peanuts
> 1 teaspoon vanilla extract

1. In heavy saucepan over medium heat, cook EAGLE BRAND® and peanut butter over medium heat just until bubbly, stirring constantly. Remove from heat; stir in white chocolate until smooth. Immediately stir in peanuts and vanilla. Spread evenly into wax paper-lined 8- or 9-inch square baking pan. Cool.

2. Cover. Chill 2 hours or until firm. Turn fudge onto cutting board; peel off paper and cut into squares. Store leftovers covered in refrigerator.

Makes about 2 1/4 pounds fudge

white truffles

2 pounds vanilla-flavored candy coating*
1 (14-ounce) can EAGLE BRAND® Sweetened Condensed Milk
  (NOT evaporated milk)
1 tablespoon vanilla extract
1 pound chocolate-flavored candy coating,* melted, or
  unsweetened cocoa

*Also called confectioners' coating. If it is not available in your local supermarket, it can be purchased in candy specialty stores.

1. In heavy saucepan over low heat, melt candy coating with EAGLE BRAND®. Remove from heat; stir in vanilla. Cool.

2. Shape into 1-inch balls. With toothpick, partially dip each ball into melted chocolate candy coating or roll in cocoa. Place on wax paper-lined baking sheets until firm. Store leftovers covered in refrigerator.   *Makes about 8 dozen truffles*

Prep Time: 40 minutes

flavoring options: Amaretto: Omit vanilla. Add 3 tablespoons amaretto or other almond-flavored liqueur and ½ teaspoon almond extract. Roll in finely chopped toasted almonds. **Orange:** Omit vanilla. Add 3 tablespoons orange-flavored liqueur. Roll in finely chopped toasted almonds mixed with finely grated orange rind. **Rum:** Omit vanilla. Add ¼ cup dark rum. Roll in flaked coconut. **Bourbon:** Omit vanilla. Add 3 tablespoons bourbon. Roll in finely chopped toasted nuts.

peppermint chocolate fudge

(pictured at right)

 2 cups (12 ounces) milk chocolate chips
 1 cup (6 ounces) semisweet chocolate chips
 1 (14-ounce) can EAGLE BRAND® Sweetened Condensed Milk
   (NOT evaporated milk)
   Dash salt
 1/2 teaspoon peppermint extract
 1/4 cup crushed hard peppermint candy

1. In heavy saucepan over low heat, melt chocolate chips with EAGLE BRAND® and salt. Remove from heat; stir in peppermint extract. Spread evenly in wax paper-lined 8- or 9-inch square pan. Sprinkle with peppermint candy.

2. Chill 2 hours or until firm. Turn fudge onto cutting board; peel off paper and cut into squares. Store leftovers covered in refrigerator.

Makes about 2 pounds fudge

Prep Time: 15 minutes
Chill Time: 2 hours

white christmas jewel fudge

 3 cups premium white chocolate chips
 1 (14-ounce) can EAGLE BRAND® Sweetened Condensed Milk
   (NOT evaporated milk)
 1 1/2 teaspoons vanilla extract
   Dash salt
 1/2 cup chopped green candied cherries
 1/2 cup chopped red candied cherries

1. In large heavy saucepan over low heat, melt chocolate chips with EAGLE BRAND®, vanilla and salt. Remove from heat; stir in cherries. Spread evenly in wax paper-lined 8- or 9-inch square pan.

2. Chill 2 hours or until firm. Turn fudge onto cutting board; peel off paper and cut into squares. Store leftovers covered in refrigerator.

Makes 2 1/4 pounds fudge

Prep Time: 15 minutes
Chill Time: 2 hours

peanut butter blocks

1 (14-ounce) can EAGLE BRAND® Sweetened Condensed Milk
   (NOT evaporated milk)
1¼ cups creamy peanut butter
⅓ cup water
1 tablespoon vanilla extract
½ teaspoon salt
1 cup cornstarch, sifted
1 pound vanilla-flavored candy coating*
2 cups peanuts, finely chopped

Also called confectioners' coating or almond bark. If it is not available in your local supermarket, it can be purchased in candy specialty stores.

1. In medium heavy saucepan, combine EAGLE BRAND®, peanut butter, water, vanilla and salt; stir in cornstarch. Over medium heat, cook and stir until thickened and smooth. Add candy coating; cook and stir until melted and smooth. Spread evenly in wax paper-lined 9-inch square baking pan.

2. Chill 2 hours or until firm. Turn candy onto cutting board; peel off paper and cut into squares. Roll firmly in peanuts to coat. Store leftovers covered at room temperature or in refrigerator.

Makes about 3 pounds candy

Prep Time: 15 minutes
Chill Time: 2 hours

microwave method: In 1-quart glass measure, combine EAGLE BRAND®, peanut butter, water, vanilla and salt; stir in cornstarch. Microwave on HIGH (100% power) 2 minutes; mix well. In 2-quart glass measure, melt candy coating on MEDIUM (50% power) 3 to 5 minutes, stirring after each minute. Add peanut butter mixture; mix well. Proceed as directed above.

no-bake peanutty chocolate drops

(pictured at right)

$\frac{1}{2}$ cup (1 stick) butter or margarine
$\frac{1}{3}$ cup unsweetened cocoa
2$\frac{1}{2}$ cups quick-cooking oats
1 (14-ounce) can EAGLE BRAND® Sweetened Condensed Milk
(NOT evaporated milk)
1 cup chopped peanuts
$\frac{1}{2}$ cup peanut butter

1. In medium saucepan over medium heat, melt butter; stir in cocoa. Bring mixture to a boil. Remove from heat; stir in oats, EAGLE BRAND®, peanuts and peanut butter.

2. Drop by teaspoonfuls onto wax paper-lined baking sheets. Chill 2 hours or until set. Store leftovers loosely covered in refrigerator.

Makes about 5 dozen drops

chocolate raspberry truffles

(pictured on page 35)

1 (14-ounce) can EAGLE BRAND® Sweetened Condensed Milk
(NOT evaporated milk)
$\frac{1}{4}$ cup raspberry liqueur
2 tablespoons butter or margarine
2 tablespoons seedless raspberry jam
2 cups (12 ounces) semisweet chocolate chips
$\frac{1}{2}$ cup powdered sugar or finely chopped toasted almonds

Microwave Directions

1. In large microwave-safe bowl, combine EAGLE BRAND®, liqueur, butter and jam. Microwave on HIGH (100% power) 3 minutes.

2. Stir in chocolate chips until smooth. Cover and chill 1 hour.

3. Shape mixture into 1-inch balls; roll in powdered sugar or almonds. Store leftovers covered at room temperature.   *Makes 4 dozen truffles*

rocky road candy

(pictured on page 87)

> 2 cups (12 ounces) semisweet chocolate chips
> 2 tablespoons butter or margarine
> 1 (14-ounce) can EAGLE BRAND® Sweetened Condensed Milk
>   (NOT evaporated milk)
> 2 cups dry-roasted peanuts
> 1 (10½-ounce) package miniature marshmallows

1. In large heavy saucepan over low heat, melt chocolate chips and butter with EAGLE BRAND®; remove from heat.

2. In large bowl, combine peanuts and marshmallows; stir in chocolate mixture. Spread in wax paper-lined 13×9-inch baking pan.

3. Chill 2 hours or until firm. Remove candy from pan; peel off paper and cut into squares. Store leftovers loosely covered at room temperature.

Makes about 3½ dozen candies

Prep Time: 10 minutes
Chill Time: 2 hours

microwave method: In 1-quart glass measure, combine chocolate chips, butter and EAGLE BRAND®. Cook on HIGH (100% power) 3 minutes, stirring after 1½ minutes. Let stand 5 minutes. Proceed as directed above.

To make cutting the candy easier, run hot water over a sharp knife and wipe it dry. Then cut into squares with a back-and-forth sawing motion.

chocolate truffles

3 cups (18 ounces) semisweet chocolate chips
1 (14-ounce) can EAGLE BRAND® Sweetened Condensed Milk
    (NOT evaporated milk)
1 tablespoon vanilla extract
    Coatings: finely chopped toasted nuts, flaked coconut,
        chocolate sprinkles, colored sugar, unsweetened cocoa,
        confectioners' sugar or colored sprinkles

1. In large saucepan over low heat, melt chocolate chips with EAGLE BRAND®. Remove from heat; stir in vanilla.

2. Pour into medium bowl, cover and chill 2 to 3 hours or until firm.

3. Shape into 1-inch balls; roll in desired coating. Chill 1 hour or until firm. Store leftovers covered in refrigerator.

Makes about 6 dozen truffles

Prep Time: 10 minutes
Chill Time: 3 hours

microwave directions: In 1-quart glass measure, combine chocolate chips and EAGLE BRAND®. Microwave at HIGH (100% power) 3 minutes, stirring after 1½ minutes. Stir until smooth. Proceed as directed above.

amaretto truffles: Substitute 3 tablespoons amaretto liqueur and ½ teaspoon almond extract for vanilla. Roll in finely chopped toasted almonds.

orange truffles: Substitute 3 tablespoons orange-flavored liqueur for vanilla. Roll in finely chopped toasted almonds mixed with finely grated orange peel.

rum truffles: Substitute ¼ cup dark rum for vanilla. Roll in flaked coconut.

bourbon truffles: Substitute 3 tablespoons bourbon for vanilla. Roll in finely chopped toasted nuts.

strawberries & cream dessert

1 (14-ounce) can EAGLE BRAND® Sweetened Condensed Milk
   (NOT evaporated milk)
1½ cups cold water
1 (4 serving-size) package instant vanilla pudding and pie
   filling mix
2 cups (1 pint) whipping cream, whipped
1 (12-ounce) prepared loaf pound cake, cut into cubes
   (about 6 cups cubes)
4 cups sliced fresh strawberries
½ cup strawberry preserves
   Additional sliced fresh strawberries
   Toasted slivered almonds*

*To toast almonds, spread in single layer in heavy-bottomed skillet. Cook over medium heat 2 to 3 minutes, stirring frequently, until nuts are lightly browned. Remove from skillet immediately. Cool before using.

1. In large bowl, combine EAGLE BRAND® and water; mix well. Add pudding mix; beat until well blended. Chill 5 minutes. Fold in whipped cream.

2. Spoon 2 cups pudding mixture into 4-quart round glass serving bowl; top with half the cake cubes, half the strawberries, half the preserves and half the remaining pudding mixture. Repeat layers of cake cubes, strawberries and preserves; top with remaining pudding mixture.

3. Garnish with additional strawberries and almonds. Chill 4 hours or until set. Store leftovers covered in refrigerator.

Makes 10 to 12 servings

Prep Time: 20 minutes
Chill Time: 4 hours 5 minutes

variation: Here is another way to layer this spectacular dessert: Spoon 2 cups pudding mixture into 4-quart round glass serving bowl; top with cake cubes, all of the strawberries, all of the preserves and the remaining pudding mixture. Garnish and chill as directed above.

chocolate mousse & raspberries

4 (1-ounce) squares unsweetened chocolate
1 (14-ounce) can EAGLE BRAND® Sweetened Condensed Milk
    (NOT evaporated milk)
2 teaspoons vanilla extract
2 cups (1 pint) whipping cream, whipped
²/₃ cup water
¼ cup red raspberry jam
3 tablespoons powdered sugar
1 tablespoon cornstarch
1 cup frozen raspberries

1. In large heavy saucepan over medium-low heat, melt chocolate with EAGLE BRAND®; stir in vanilla. Pour into large bowl; cool to room temperature, about 1½ hours.

2. Beat chocolate mixture until smooth. Fold in whipped cream. Spoon into 8 to 10 individual dessert dishes. Chill.

3. In small saucepan, combine water, jam, powdered sugar and cornstarch. Cook and stir until thickened and clear. Cool. Stir in raspberries.

4. Top each serving with raspberry topping and serve. Store leftovers covered in refrigerator.   *Makes 8 to 10 servings*

Prep Time: 10 minutes

Jam is a sweet, thick spread made from crushed fruit cooked with sugar. It is similar to preserves in how it is made, but unlike preserves, it seldom contains fruit pieces that are big enough to be identified.

hot fudge sauce

1 cup (6 ounces) semisweet chocolate chips *or* 4 (1-ounce)
    squares semisweet chocolate
2 tablespoons butter or margarine
1 (14-ounce) can EAGLE BRAND® Sweetened Condensed Milk
    (NOT evaporated milk)
2 tablespoons water
1 teaspoon vanilla extract

1. In medium heavy saucepan over medium heat, melt chocolate chips and butter with EAGLE BRAND® and water. Cook and stir constantly until smooth. Stir in vanilla.

2. Serve warm over cream puffs or as dipping sauce for fruit. Store leftovers covered in refrigerator.   *Makes 2 cups sauce*

Prep Time: 10 minutes

spirited hot fudge sauce: Add ¼ cup almond-, coffee-, mint- or orange-flavored liqueur with vanilla.

dulce de leche

1 (14-ounce) can EAGLE BRAND® Sweetened Condensed Milk
    (NOT evaporated milk)
Assorted dippers, such as cookies, pound cake cubes, angel
    food cake cubes, banana chunks orange slices, apple slices

1. Preheat oven to 425°F. Pour EAGLE BRAND® into ungreased 9-inch pie plate. Cover with foil; place in larger shallow baking pan. Pour hot water into larger pan to depth of 1 inch.

2. Bake 1 hour or until thick and caramel-colored. Beat until smooth. Cool 1 hour. Refrigerate until serving time. Serve as dip with assorted dippers. Store leftovers covered in refrigerator for up to 1 week.
    Makes about 1½ cups dip

Prep Time: 5 minutes
Bake Time: 1 hour
Cool Time: 1 hour

caution: Never heat an unopened can.

creamy banana pudding

(pictured at right)

   1 (14-ounce) can EAGLE BRAND® Sweetened Condensed Milk
      (NOT evaporated milk)
1½ cups cold water
   1 (4 serving-size) package instant vanilla pudding and pie
      filling mix
   2 cups (1 pint) whipping cream, whipped
 36 vanilla wafers
   3 medium bananas, sliced and dipped in lemon juice

1. In large bowl, combine EAGLE BRAND® and water. Add pudding mix; beat until well blended. Chill 5 minutes.

2. Fold in whipped cream. Spoon 1 cup pudding mixture among 8 to 10 individual serving dishes.

3. Top with one-third each vanilla wafers, bananas and pudding mixture. Repeat layers twice, ending with pudding mixture. Chill. Garnish as desired. Store leftovers covered in refrigerator.

Makes 8 to 10 servings

Prep Time: 15 minutes

dipsy doodles butterscotch dip

   1 (14-ounce) can EAGLE BRAND® Sweetened Condensed Milk
      (NOT evaporated milk)
1½ cups milk
   1 (4 serving-size) package cook-and-serve butterscotch pudding
      and pie filling mix
   Apples or pears, cored and sliced, or banana chunks

1. In medium saucepan over medium heat, combine EAGLE BRAND®, milk and pudding mix. Cook and stir until thickened and bubbly; cook 2 minutes more. Cool slightly.

2. Pour into serving bowl. Serve warm with fruit.

Makes about 2½ cups dip

Prep Time: 15 minutes

holiday cheese tarts

(pictured at right)

> 1 (8-ounce) package cream cheese, softened
> 1 (14-ounce) can EAGLE BRAND® Sweetened Condensed Milk
>   (NOT evaporated milk)
> 1/3 cup lemon juice
> 1 teaspoon vanilla extract
> 2 (4-ounce) packages single-serve graham cracker crumb crusts
>   Assorted fruit (strawberries, blueberries, raspberries, orange
>   segments, cherries, kiwifruit, grapes and/or pineapple)
> 1/4 cup apple jelly, melted (optional)

1. In large bowl, beat cream cheese until fluffy. Gradually beat in EAGLE BRAND® until smooth. Stir in lemon juice and vanilla; mix well. Pour into crusts.

2. Chill 2 hours or until set. Just before serving, top with fruit; brush with jelly (optional). Store leftovers covered in refrigerator.

Makes 1 dozen tarts

s'mores on a stick

> 1 (14-ounce) can EAGLE BRAND® Sweetened Condensed Milk
>   (NOT evaporated milk), divided
> 1 1/2 cups miniature milk chocolate chips, divided
> 1 cup miniature marshmallows
> 11 whole graham crackers, halved crosswise
>   Toppings: chopped peanuts, miniature candy-coated chocolate
>   pieces and/or sprinkles

1. In microwave-safe bowl, microwave half of EAGLE BRAND® at HIGH (100% power) 1 1/2 minutes. Stir in 1 cup chocolate chips until smooth; stir in marshmallows.

2. Spread chocolate mixture evenly by heaping tablespoonfuls onto 11 graham cracker halves. Top with remaining graham cracker halves; place on wax paper.

3. Microwave remaining EAGLE BRAND® at HIGH (100% power) 1 1/2 minutes; stir in remaining 1/2 cup chocolate chips, stirring until smooth. Drizzle mixture over treats; sprinkle with desired toppings. Let stand for 2 hours; insert wooden craft stick into centers.

Makes 11 treats

chocolate peanut butter dessert sauce

(pictured at right)

> 2 (1-ounce) squares semisweet chocolate, chopped
> 2 tablespoons creamy peanut butter
> 1 (14-ounce) can EAGLE BRAND® Sweetened Condensed Milk
>   (NOT evaporated milk)
> 2 tablespoons milk
> 1 teaspoon vanilla extract
>   Fresh fruit, ice cream or cake

1. In medium saucepan over medium-low heat, melt chocolate and peanut butter with EAGLE BRAND® and milk, stirring constantly. Remove from heat; stir in vanilla. Cool slightly.

2. Serve warm as fruit dipping sauce or over ice cream or cake. Store leftovers covered in refrigerator. *Makes about 1½ cups sauce*

chocolate cream crêpes

> 1 (14-ounce) can EAGLE BRAND® Sweetened Condensed Milk
>   (NOT evaporated milk)
> ¼ cup cold water
> 1 (4 serving-size) package instant chocolate pudding and pie
>   filling mix
> ¼ cup unsweetened cocoa
> 1 cup (½ pint) whipping cream, whipped
> 1 (4½-ounce) package ready-to-use crêpes (10 crêpes)
> 1½ cups sliced or cut-up fresh fruit such as strawberries, peaches,
>   nectarines, raspberries or kiwifruit
>   Powdered sugar
>   White chocolate curls (optional)

1. In large bowl with electric mixer at medium speed, beat EAGLE BRAND® and water. Beat in pudding mix and cocoa. Fold in whipped cream. Cover and chill 15 minutes.

2. Pipe or spoon ⅓ cup filling down center of crêpes. Roll up crêpes. Place on serving plates. Spoon fruit over crêpes. Sprinkle with powdered sugar. Garnish with white chocolate curls (optional). Store leftovers covered in refrigerator. *Makes 5 servings*

cherry-berry crumble

(pictured at right)

1 (21-ounce) can cherry pie filling
2 cups fresh or frozen raspberries
1 (14-ounce) can EAGLE BRAND® Sweetened Condensed Milk
 (NOT evaporated milk)
1¹/₂ cups granola

1. In medium saucepan over medium heat, cook and stir cherry pie filling and raspberries until heated through. Stir in EAGLE BRAND®; cook and stir 1 minute.

2. Spoon into 6 ungreased individual dessert dishes. Sprinkle with granola; garnish as desired. Serve warm. Store leftovers covered in refrigerator. *Makes 6 servings*

cherry-rhubarb crumble: Substitute fresh or frozen sliced rhubarb for raspberries. In medium saucepan over medium-high heat, cook and stir pie filling and rhubarb until bubbly. Cook and stir 5 minutes more. Proceed as directed above.

no-bake fudgy brownies

1 (14-ounce) can EAGLE BRAND® Sweetened Condensed Milk
 (NOT evaporated milk)
2 (1-ounce) squares unsweetened chocolate, chopped
1 teaspoon vanilla extract
2 cups plus 2 tablespoons finely crushed chocolate wafer
 cookies, divided (about 25 cookies)
¹/₄ cup miniature candy-coated milk chocolate pieces

1. In medium saucepan over low heat, combine EAGLE BRAND® and chocolate; cook and stir just until boiling. Reduce heat; cook and stir for 2 to 3 minutes more or until mixture thickens. Remove from heat; stir in vanilla.

2. Stir in 2 cups cookie crumbs. Spread evenly in foil-lined 8-inch square baking pan. Sprinkle with remaining cookie crumbs and chocolate pieces; press down gently with back of spoon.

3. Cover and chill 4 hours or until firm. Turn brownies onto cutting board; peel off foil and cut into squares. Store leftovers covered in refrigerator. *Makes 2 to 3 dozen brownies*

tiramisu

   2 tablespoons instant coffee
   ½ cup hot water
   2 (3-ounce) packages ladyfingers (24 each), cut crosswise into
      quarters
   1 (14-ounce) can EAGLE BRAND® Sweetened Condensed Milk
      (NOT evaporated milk), divided
   1 package (8 ounces) cream cheese or mascarpone cheese,
      softened
   2 cups (1 pint) whipping cream, divided
   1 teaspoon vanilla extract
   1 cup (6 ounces) miniature semisweet chocolate chips, divided
      Grated semisweet chocolate and/or strawberries (optional)

1. In small bowl, dissolve coffee in water; reserve 1 tablespoon coffee mixture. Brush remaining coffee mixture on cut sides of ladyfingers; set aside.

2. In large bowl, beat ¾ cup EAGLE BRAND® and cream cheese. Add 1¼ cups whipping cream, vanilla and reserved 1 tablespoon coffee mixture; beat until soft peaks form. Fold in ½ cup chocolate chips.

3. In small heavy saucepan over low heat, melt remaining ½ cup chocolate chips with remaining EAGLE BRAND®.

4. In 8 individual tall dessert glasses or parfait glasses, layer cream cheese mixture, chocolate mixture and ladyfinger pieces, beginning and ending with cream cheese mixture. Cover and chill at least 4 hours.

5. In medium bowl, beat remaining ¾ cup whipping cream until soft peaks form. Spoon whipped cream over dessert. Garnish as desired. Store leftovers covered in refrigerator.   *Makes 8 servings*

Prep Time: 30 minutes
Chill Time: 4 hours

creamy rice pudding

(pictured at right)

  1 1/2 **cups water**
   1/2 **cup long grain rice***
    1 **cinnamon stick**
    1 **(1-inch) piece orange or lemon rind**
      Dash salt
    1 **(14-ounce) can EAGLE BRAND® Sweetened Condensed Milk**
      (NOT evaporated milk)
   1/2 **cup raisins or pecan halves (optional)**
      Ground cinnamon

*DO NOT use quick-cooking rice.

1. In medium saucepan, combine water, rice, cinnamon stick, orange rind and salt. Bring to a boil; reduce heat. Cover and simmer 15 minutes.

2. Stir in EAGLE BRAND®. Cook uncovered over low heat, stirring frequently 25 minutes or until rice is tender. (Mixture will thicken as it cools.) Remove cinnamon stick and orange rind. Cool. Stir in raisins or pecans (optional).

3. Spoon pudding into 4 individual serving dishes. Garnish with cinnamon. Serve warm or chilled. Store leftovers covered in refrigerator.

Makes 4 servings

fudgy milk chocolate fondue

    1 **(16-ounce) can chocolate syrup**
    1 **(14-ounce) can EAGLE BRAND® Sweetened Condensed Milk**
      (NOT evaporated milk)
      Dash salt
  1 1/2 **teaspoons vanilla extract**
      Assorted dippers: cookies, cake cubes, fruit slices and/or
      marshmallows

1. In heavy saucepan over medium heat, combine chocolate syrup, EAGLE BRAND® and salt. Cook and stir 12 to 15 minutes or until slightly thickened. Remove from heat; stir in vanilla.

2. Serve warm with assorted dippers. Store leftovers covered in refrigerator.

Makes about 3 cups fondue

tasty beverages

festive cranberry cream punch

Cranberry Ice Ring (recipe follows) or ice
1 (14-ounce) can EAGLE BRAND® Sweetened Condensed Milk
   (NOT evaporated milk)
1 (12-ounce) can frozen cranberry juice cocktail concentrate,
   thawed
1 cup cranberry-flavored liqueur (optional)
Red food coloring (optional)
2 (1-liter) bottles club soda or ginger ale, chilled

1. Prepare Cranberry Ice Ring one day in advance.

2. In punch bowl, combine EAGLE BRAND®, cranberry concentrate, liqueur (optional) and food coloring (optional).

3. Just before serving, add club soda and Cranberry Ice Ring or ice. Store tightly covered in refrigerator. *Makes about 3 quarts punch*

cranberry ice ring

2 cups cranberry juice cocktail
1½ cups water
¾ to 1 cup cranberries and lime slices or mint leaves

1. Combine cranberry juice cocktail and water in large bowl. In 1½-quart ring mold, pour ½ cup cranberry mixture. Arrange cranberries and lime slices or mint leaves in mold; freeze.

2. Add remaining 3 cups cranberry liquid to mold; freeze overnight.
Makes 1 ice ring

strawberry splash punch

(pictured at right)

> 1¹/₂ cups fresh whole strawberries
> ¹/₂ cup lemon juice, chilled
> 1 (14-ounce) can EAGLE BRAND® Sweetened Condensed Milk
>   (NOT evaporated milk), chilled
> 1 (1-liter) bottle strawberry carbonated beverage, chilled
>   Ice cubes (optional)
>   Fresh whole strawberries (optional)

1. In blender container, combine 1¹/₂ cups strawberries and lemon juice; cover and blend until smooth. Add EAGLE BRAND®; cover and blend. Pour into large pitcher.

2. Gradually stir in carbonated beverage. Add ice (optional). Garnish each serving with whole strawberry (optional).   *Makes 10 servings*

Prep Time: 10 minutes

banana smoothies

> 1 (14-ounce) can EAGLE BRAND® Sweetened Condensed Milk
>   (NOT evaporated milk)
> 1 (8-ounce) container vanilla yogurt
> 2 ripe bananas, sliced
> ¹/₂ cup orange juice

1. In blender container, combine EAGLE BRAND®, yogurt, bananas and juice; blend until smooth, scraping sides occasionally.

2. Serve immediately. Store leftovers covered in refrigerator.

Makes 4 cups

Prep Time: 5 minutes

banana smoothie pops: Spoon banana mixture into 8 (5-ounce) paper cups. Freeze 30 minutes. Insert wooden craft sticks into center of each cup; freeze until firm. Makes 8 pops.

fruit smoothies: Substitute 1 cup of your favorite fruit and ¹/₂ cup any fruit juice for banana and orange juice.

chilled café latte

> **2 tablespoons** instant coffee
> **³/₄ cup** warm water
> **1 (14-ounce) can** EAGLE BRAND® Sweetened Condensed Milk (NOT evaporated milk)
> **1 teaspoon** vanilla extract
> **4 cups** ice cubes

1. In blender container, dissolve coffee in water. Add EAGLE BRAND® and vanilla; cover and blend on high speed until smooth.

2. With blender running, gradually add ice cubes, blending until smooth. Serve immediately. Store leftovers covered in refrigerator.

Makes about 5 cups

Prep Time: 10 minutes

A café latte is an espresso with steamed milk served in a tall mug topped with the foam of the steamed milk. In warmer weather, this recipe provides a great alternative to a hot latte.

fruit smoothies

1 (14-ounce) can EAGLE BRAND® Sweetened Condensed Milk
   (NOT evaporated milk), chilled
1 (8-ounce) container plain yogurt
1 small banana, cut up
1 cup fresh or frozen whole strawberries
1 (8-ounce) can crushed pineapple packed in juice, chilled
2 tablespoons lemon juice
1 cup ice cubes
   Additional fresh strawberries (optional)

1. In blender container, combine chilled EAGLE BRAND®, yogurt, banana, strawberries, pineapple with its juice and lemon juice; cover and blend until smooth. With blender running, gradually add ice cubes, blending until smooth.

2. Garnish with strawberries (optional). Serve immediately.

Makes 5 servings

Prep Time: 5 minutes

peach smoothies: Omit strawberries and pineapple. Add 2 cups fresh or frozen sliced peaches. Proceed as directed above.

key lime smoothies: Omit strawberries, pineapple and lemon juice. Add ⅓ cup key lime juice from concentrate. Proceed as directed above. Tint with green food coloring and garnish with lime slices, if desired.

creamy hot chocolate

1 (14-ounce) can EAGLE BRAND® Sweetened Condensed Milk
   (NOT evaporated milk)
½ cup unsweetened cocoa powder
1½ teaspoons vanilla extract
   Dash salt
6½ cups water
   Miniature marshmallows (optional)

1. In large saucepan over medium heat, combine EAGLE BRAND®, cocoa, vanilla and salt; mix well. Slowly stir in water. Heat through, stirring occasionally. Do not boil.

2. Top with marshmallows (optional). Store leftovers covered in refrigerator. *Makes about 8 cups hot chocolate*

Prep Time: 8 to 10 minutes

microwave method: In 2-quart glass measure, combine all ingredients except marshmallows. Microwave on HIGH (100% power) 8 to 10 minutes, stirring every 3 minutes. Top with marshmallows (optional).

homemade irish cream liqueur

- 2 cups whipping cream or coffee cream
- 1 (14-ounce) can EAGLE BRAND® Sweetened Condensed Milk (NOT evaporated milk)
- 1¼ to 1¾ cups Irish whiskey, brandy, rum, bourbon, Scotch or rye whiskey
- 2 tablespoons chocolate syrup
- 2 teaspoons instant coffee
- 1 teaspoon vanilla extract
- ½ teaspoon almond extract

1. In blender container, combine whipping cream, EAGLE BRAND®, whiskey, chocolate syrup, coffee, vanilla and almond extract; blend until smooth.

2. Serve over ice. Store leftovers tightly covered in refrigerator.

Makes about 5 cups

Prep Time: 5 minutes

homemade cream liqueur: Omit Irish whiskey, chocolate syrup, coffee and extracts. Add 1¼ cups flavored liqueur (almond, coffee, orange or mint) to EAGLE BRAND® and cream. Proceed as directed above.

For a more blended flavor, store the homemade liqueur in the refrigerator for several hours before serving.

happy endings

blueberry streusel cobbler

1 pint fresh or frozen blueberries
1 (14-ounce) can EAGLE BRAND® Sweetened Condensed Milk
   (NOT evaporated milk)
2 teaspoons grated lemon rind
³/₄ cup (1¹/₂ sticks) plus 2 tablespoons cold butter or margarine,
   divided
2 cups biscuit baking mix, divided
¹/₂ cup firmly packed brown sugar
¹/₂ cup chopped nuts
   Vanilla ice cream
   Blueberry Sauce (recipe follows)

1. Preheat oven to 325°F.

2. In medium bowl, combine blueberries, EAGLE BRAND® and lemon rind.

3. In large bowl, cut ³/₄ cup (1¹/₂ sticks) butter into 1¹/₂ cups biscuit mix until crumbly; stir in blueberry mixture. Spread in greased 9-inch square baking pan.

4. In small bowl, combine remaining ¹/₂ cup biscuit mix and brown sugar; cut in remaining 2 tablespoons butter until crumbly. Stir in nuts. Sprinkle over batter.

5. Bake 65 to 70 minutes. Serve warm with vanilla ice cream and Blueberry Sauce. Store leftovers covered in refrigerator.

Makes 8 to 12 servings

blueberry sauce

¹/₂ cup sugar
1 tablespoon cornstarch
¹/₂ teaspoon ground cinnamon
¹/₄ teaspoon ground nutmeg
¹/₂ cup water
1 pint blueberries

1. In saucepan over medium heat, combine sugar, cornstarch, cinnamon and nutmeg. Gradually add water. Cook and stir until thickened. Stir in blueberries; cook and stir until hot.

Makes about 1²/₃ cups

marbled cheesecake bars

2 cups finely crushed chocolate crème-filled sandwich cookies
    (about 24 cookies)
3 tablespoons butter or margarine, melted
3 (8-ounce) packages cream cheese, softened
1 (14-ounce) can EAGLE BRAND® Sweetened Condensed Milk
    (NOT evaporated milk)
3 eggs
2 teaspoons vanilla extract
2 (1-ounce) squares unsweetened chocolate, melted

1. Preheat oven to 300°F. In medium bowl, combine cookie crumbs and butter; press firmly on bottom of 13×9-inch baking pan.

2. In large bowl, beat cream cheese until fluffy. Gradually beat in EAGLE BRAND® until smooth. Add eggs and vanilla; mix well. Pour half the batter evenly into crust.

3. Stir melted chocolate into remaining batter; spoon over vanilla batter. With knife or metal spatula, gently swirl through batters to marble.

4. Bake 40 to 50 minutes or until set. Cool. Chill. Cut into bars. Store leftovers covered in refrigerator. *Makes 2 to 3 dozen bars*

Prep Time: 20 minutes
Bake Time: 45 to 50 minutes

dutch apple dessert

  5 medium apples, peeled, cored and sliced
  1 (14-ounce) can EAGLE BRAND® Sweetened Condensed Milk
      (NOT evaporated milk)
  1 teaspoon ground cinnamon
  ½ cup (1 stick) plus 2 tablespoons cold butter or margarine,
      divided
1½ cups biscuit baking mix, divided
  ½ cup firmly packed brown sugar
  ½ cup chopped nuts
      Ice cream (optional)

1. Preheat oven to 325°F.

2. In medium bowl, combine apples, EAGLE BRAND® and cinnamon.

3. In large bowl, cut ½ cup (1 stick) butter into 1 cup biscuit mix until crumbly. Stir in apple mixture. Pour into greased 9-inch square baking pan.

4. In small bowl, combine remaining ½ cup biscuit mix and brown sugar. Cut in 2 tablespoons butter until crumbly; add nuts. Sprinkle evenly over apple mixture.

5. Bake 1 hour or until golden. Serve warm with ice cream (optional). Store leftovers covered in refrigerator.   *Makes 6 to 8 servings*

Prep Time: 25 minutes

microwave method: In 2-quart round baking dish, prepare as directed above. Microwave on HIGH (100% power) 14 to 15 minutes, rotating dish after 7 minutes. Let stand 5 minutes.

two-tone cheesecake bars

　　2 cups finely crushed crème-filled chocolate sandwich cookies
　　　　(about 24 cookies)
　　3 tablespoons butter or margarine, melted
　　3 (8-ounce) packages cream cheese, softened
　　1 (14-ounce) can EAGLE BRAND® Sweetened Condensed Milk
　　　　(NOT evaporated milk)
　　3 eggs
　　2 teaspoons vanilla extract
　　2 (1-ounce) squares unsweetened chocolate, melted
　　　Chocolate Glaze (recipe follows)

1. Preheat oven to 300°F. In medium bowl, combine cookie crumbs and butter; press firmly on bottom of ungreased 13×9-inch baking pan.

2. In large bowl, beat cream cheese until fluffy. Gradually beat in EAGLE BRAND® until smooth. Add eggs and vanilla; mix well. Pour half the batter evenly over crust. Stir melted chocolate into remaining batter; spoon evenly over plain batter.

3. Bake 55 to 60 minutes or until set. Cool. Top with Chocolate Glaze. Chill. Cut into bars. Store leftovers covered in refrigerator.

Makes 2 to 3 dozen bars

Prep Time: 15 minutes
Bake Time: 55 to 60 minutes

chocolate glaze

　　2 (1-ounce) squares unsweetened chocolate
　　2 tablespoons butter or margarine
　　　Dash salt
　1¾ cups powdered sugar
　　3 tablespoons hot water or cream

1. In heavy saucepan over low heat, melt chocolate and butter with salt. Remove from heat. Add powdered sugar and hot water or cream; mix well. Immediately spread over cheesecake.　　*Makes about 1 cup*

golden bread pudding

4 cups soft white bread cubes (about 5 slices)
3 eggs
1 teaspoon ground cinnamon
3 cups warm water
1 (14-ounce) can EAGLE BRAND® Sweetened Condensed Milk
   (NOT evaporated milk)
2 tablespoons butter or margarine, melted
2 teaspoons vanilla extract
1/2 teaspoon salt
  Butter Rum Sauce (recipe follows)

1. Preheat oven to 350°F. Place bread cubes in buttered 9-inch square baking pan.

2. In large bowl, beat eggs and cinnamon. Beat in water, EAGLE BRAND® butter, vanilla and salt until smooth. Pour evenly over bread cubes, moistening completely.

3. Bake 45 to 50 minutes or until knife inserted near center comes out clean. Cool slightly. Serve warm with Butter Rum Sauce. Store leftovers covered in refrigerator. *Makes 6 to 9 servings*

Prep Time: 15 minutes
Bake Time: 45 to 50 minutes

butter rum sauce

1/4 cup (1/2 stick) butter or margarine
3/4 cup firmly packed brown sugar
1/2 cup whipping cream
2 tablespoons rum *or* 1 teaspoon rum flavoring

1. In medium saucepan over medium-high heat, melt butter; add brown sugar and whipping cream. Boil rapidly 8 to 10 minutes; add rum. Serve warm. *Makes about 1 cup*

citrus-filled meringues

8 (3-inch) Meringue Shells (recipe follows)
1 (14-ounce) can EAGLE BRAND® Sweetened Condensed Milk
    (NOT evaporated milk)
$^{1}/_{2}$ cup frozen limeade concentrate, thawed
2 tablespoons lemon juice
2 egg yolks
    Green or yellow food coloring (optional)
1 (4-ounce) container frozen nondairy whipped topping,
    thawed (about $1^{3}/_{4}$ cups)

1. Prepare Meringue Shells in advance.

2. In medium saucepan, combine EAGLE BRAND®, limeade, lemon juice and egg yolks; mix well. Over medium heat, cook and stir rapidly until hot and slightly thickened. Remove from heat; cool 15 minutes. Chill. Stir in food coloring (optional). Fold in whipped topping.

3. Chill until ready to serve. Spoon into Meringue Shells just before serving. Garnish as desired. Store leftovers covered in refrigerator.

Makes 8 servings

meringue shells

3 egg whites, at room temperature
1 teaspoon vanilla extract
$^{1}/_{4}$ teaspoon cream of tartar
$^{1}/_{4}$ teaspoon salt
$^{3}/_{4}$ cup sugar

1. Preheat oven to 250°F. Cover baking sheets with parchment paper. Draw 8 (3-inch) circles about 2 inches apart on paper; set aside.

2. In large bowl, combine egg whites, vanilla, cream of tartar and salt. Beat with electric mixer at medium speed until soft peaks form. On high speed, gradually beat in sugar until stiff but not dry. Spoon meringue within the circles on paper, forming a hollow in centers.

3. Bake 1 hour. Turn off oven; leave meringues in oven 1 hour. Cool at room temperature. Store tightly covered at room temperature.

Makes 8 shells

vanilla mint cream puffs

  12 Cream Puffs (recipe follows)
  1 (14-ounce) can EAGLE BRAND® Sweetened Condensed Milk
     (NOT evaporated milk)
  2 tablespoons white crème de menthe liqueur
  2 tablespoons cold water
  1 (4 serving-size) package instant vanilla pudding and pie
     filling mix
  1 cup (½ pint) whipping cream, whipped
    Powdered sugar
    Hot Fudge Sauce (optional, page 234)

1. Prepare Cream Puffs in advance.

2. In large bowl, combine EAGLE BRAND®, liqueur and water. Add pudding mix; beat well. Chill 5 minutes. Fold in whipped cream. Chill.

3. Just before serving, fill cream puffs; sprinkle with powdered sugar. Serve with Hot Fudge Sauce (optional). Store leftovers covered in refrigerator. *Makes 12 servings*

cream puffs

  1 cup water
  ½ cup (1 stick) butter or margarine
  1 cup all-purpose flour
  4 eggs

1. Preheat oven to 400°F.

2. In medium saucepan, heat water and butter to a rolling boil. Stir in flour. Reduce heat to low; stir rapidly until mixture forms a ball, about 1 minute. Remove from heat. Add eggs; beat until smooth. Using about ¼ cup for each puff, drop dough 3 inches apart onto ungreased baking sheets.

3. Bake 35 to 40 minutes or until puffed and golden. Cool. To serve, split and remove any dough from centers of puffs. *Makes 12 puffs*

cheesecake-topped brownies

1 (19.5- or 22-ounce) package fudge brownie mix
1 (8-ounce) package cream cheese, softened
2 tablespoons butter or margarine, softened
1 tablespoon cornstarch
1 (14-ounce) can EAGLE BRAND® Sweetened Condensed Milk
   (NOT evaporated milk)
1 egg
2 teaspoons vanilla extract
   Ready-to-spread chocolate frosting (optional)

1. Preheat oven to 350°F. Prepare brownie mix as package directs. Spread in well-greased 13×9-inch baking pan.

2. In large bowl, beat cream cheese, butter and cornstarch until fluffy. Gradually beat in EAGLE BRAND®, egg and vanilla until smooth. Spoon cheesecake mixture evenly over brownie batter.

3. Bake 45 minutes or until top is lightly browned. Cool. Spread with frosting (optional). Cut into bars. Store leftovers covered in refrigerator.   *Makes 3 to 3½ dozen brownies*

Prep Time: 20 minutes
Bake Time: 45 minutes

chocolate cinnamon bread pudding

4 cups soft white bread cubes (about 5 slices)
$^1/_2$ cup chopped nuts
3 eggs
$^1/_4$ cup unsweetened cocoa
2 teaspoons vanilla extract
1 teaspoon ground cinnamon
$^1/_2$ teaspoon salt
$2^3/_4$ cups water
1 (14-ounce) can EAGLE BRAND® Sweetened Condensed Milk
    (NOT evaporated milk)
2 tablespoons butter or margarine, melted
Cinnamon Cream Sauce (recipe follows)

1. Preheat oven to 350°F. Place bread cubes and nuts in buttered 9-inch square baking pan.

2. In large bowl, beat eggs, cocoa, vanilla, cinnamon and salt. Add water, EAGLE BRAND® and butter; mix well. Pour evenly over bread cubes, moistening completely.

3. Bake 40 to 45 minutes or until knife inserted near center comes out clean. Cool slightly. Serve warm topped with Cinnamon Cream Sauce. Store leftovers covered in refrigerator.   *Makes 6 to 9 servings*

cinnamon cream sauce

1 cup whipping cream
$^2/_3$ cup firmly packed brown sugar
1 teaspoon vanilla extract
$^1/_2$ teaspoon ground cinnamon

1. In medium saucepan over medium-high heat, combine whipping cream, brown sugar, vanilla and cinnamon. Bring to a boil; boil rapidly 6 to 8 minutes or until thickened, stirring occasionally. Serve warm.   *Makes about 1 cup*

creamy caramel flan

    ¾ **cup sugar**
    4 **eggs**
    1¾ **cups water**
    1 **(14-ounce) can EAGLE BRAND® Sweetened Condensed Milk**
        (NOT evaporated milk)
    1 **teaspoon vanilla extract**
    Dash salt
    Sugar Garnish (recipe follows, optional)

1. Preheat oven to 350°F. In medium heavy skillet over medium heat, cook and stir sugar until melted and caramel-colored. Carefully pour into 8 ungreased 6-ounce custard cups, tilting to coat bottoms.

2. In large bowl, beat eggs; stir in water, EAGLE BRAND®, vanilla and salt. Pour into custard cups. Set cups in large deep pan. Fill pan with 1 inch hot water.

3. Bake 25 minutes or until knife inserted near centers comes out clean. Move cups from pan to wire rack. Cool 1 hour. Chill several hours or overnight.

4. To serve, loosen sides of flans with knife; invert flans onto individual serving plates. Top with Sugar Garnish (optional), or as desired. Store leftovers covered in refrigerator.   *Makes 8 servings*

Prep Time: 15 minutes
Bake Time: 25 minutes

sugar garnish: Fill medium metal bowl half-full of ice. In medium saucepan over medium-high heat, combine 1 cup sugar with ¼ cup water. Stir; cover and bring to a boil. Cook over high heat 5 to 6 minutes or until light brown in color. Immediately place pan in ice for 1 minute. Using spoon, carefully drizzle sugar decoratively over foil. Cool. To serve, peel sugar garnish from foil.

french apple bread pudding

4 cups cubed French bread
½ cup raisins (optional)
3 eggs
1 (14-ounce) can EAGLE BRAND® Sweetened Condensed Milk (NOT evaporated milk)
3 medium apples, peeled, cored and finely chopped
1¾ cups hot water
¼ cup (½ stick) butter or margarine, melted
1 teaspoon ground cinnamon
1 teaspoon vanilla extract
Ice cream (optional)

1. Preheat oven to 350°F. Combine bread cubes and raisins (optional) in buttered 9-inch square baking pan.

2. In large bowl, beat eggs; add EAGLE BRAND®, apples, water, butter, cinnamon and vanilla. Pour evenly over bread and raisins, moistening completely.

3. Bake 50 to 55 minutes or until knife inserted near center comes out clean. Cool slightly. Serve warm with ice cream (optional). Store leftovers covered in refrigerator.   *Makes 6 to 9 servings*

Prep Time: 20 minutes
Bake Time: 50 to 55 minutes

Always use the type of bread called for in bread pudding recipes. Substituting a different bread may affect the amount of liquid absorbed.

creamy cinnamon rolls

2 (1-pound) loaves frozen bread dough, thawed
²/₃ cup (half of 14-ounce can*) EAGLE BRAND® Sweetened
    Condensed Milk (NOT evaporated milk), divided
1 cup chopped pecans
2 teaspoons ground cinnamon
1 cup powdered sugar
¹/₂ teaspoon vanilla extract
    Additional chopped pecans (optional)

*Use remaining EAGLE BRAND® as a dip for fruit. Pour into storage container and store tightly covered in refrigerator for up to 1 week.

1. On lightly floured surface, roll each bread dough loaf into 12×9-inch rectangle. Spread ¹/₃ cup EAGLE BRAND® over dough rectangles. Cover and chill remaining EAGLE BRAND®. Sprinkle rectangles with 1 cup pecans and cinnamon. Roll up jelly-roll style starting from short side. Cut each log into 6 slices.

2. Place rolls cut sides down in well-greased 13×9-inch baking pan. Cover loosely with greased wax paper and then with plastic wrap. Chill overnight.

3. Let pan of rolls stand at room temperature 30 minutes. Preheat oven to 350°F. Bake 30 to 35 minutes or until golden brown. Cool in pan 5 minutes; loosen edges and remove rolls from pan.

4. In small bowl, combine powdered sugar, remaining ¹/₃ cup EAGLE BRAND® and vanilla. Drizzle frosting over warm rolls. Sprinkle with additional chopped pecans (optional).   *Makes 12 rolls*

Prep Time: 20 minutes
Bake Time: 30 to 35 minutes
Cool Time: 5 minutes

index

METRIC CONVERSION CHART

VOLUME MEASUREMENTS (dry)

1/8 teaspoon = 0.5 mL
1/4 teaspoon = 1 mL
1/2 teaspoon = 2 mL
3/4 teaspoon = 4 mL
1 teaspoon = 5 mL
1 tablespoon = 15 mL
2 tablespoons = 30 mL
1/4 cup = 60 mL
1/3 cup = 75 mL
1/2 cup = 125 mL
2/3 cup = 150 mL
3/4 cup = 175 mL
1 cup = 250 mL
2 cups = 1 pint = 500 mL
3 cups = 750 mL
4 cups = 1 quart = 1 L

VOLUME MEASUREMENTS (fluid)

1 fluid ounce (2 tablespoons) = 30 mL
4 fluid ounces (1/2 cup) = 125 mL
8 fluid ounces (1 cup) = 250 mL
12 fluid ounces (1 1/2 cups) = 375 mL
16 fluid ounces (2 cups) = 500 mL

WEIGHTS (mass)

1/2 ounce = 15 g
1 ounce = 30 g
3 ounces = 90 g
4 ounces = 120 g
8 ounces = 225 g
10 ounces = 285 g
12 ounces = 360 g
16 ounces = 1 pound = 450 g

DIMENSIONS

1/16 inch = 2 mm
1/8 inch = 3 mm
1/4 inch = 6 mm
1/2 inch = 1.5 cm
3/4 inch = 2 cm
1 inch = 2.5 cm

OVEN TEMPERATURES

250°F = 120°C
275°F = 140°C
300°F = 150°C
325°F = 160°C
350°F = 180°C
375°F = 190°C
400°F = 200°C
425°F = 220°C
450°F = 230°C

BAKING PAN SIZES

Utensil	Size in Inches/Quarts	Metric Volume	Size in Centimeters
Baking or	8×8×2	2 L	20×20×5
Cake Pan	9×9×2	2.5 L	23×23×5
(square or	12×8×2	3 L	30×20×5
rectangular)	13×9×2	3.5 L	33×23×5
Loaf Pan	8×4×3	1.5 L	20×10×7
	9×5×3	2 L	23×13×7
Round Layer	8×1½	1.2 L	20×4
Cake Pan	9×1½	1.5 L	23×4
Pie Plate	8×1¼	750 mL	20×3
	9×1¼	1 L	23×3
Baking Dish	1 quart	1 L	—
or Casserole	1½ quart	1.5 L	—
	2 quart	2 L	—